S0-AAE-637

New Chinese Architecture

Editorial Staff

Senior Editor: Luo Xiaowei
Planner: Mei Di Media
Chief Editors: Zhi Wenjun, Xu Jie
Executive Editor: Dai Chun
Editors: Yao Yanbin, Guo Hongxia, Zhang Xiaochun, Ling Lin
English Editors: Xu Diyan, Liu Xiaoqiang
Graphic Designers: Ling Lin, Yao Yanbin, Guo Hongxia, Dai Chun
Graphic Operators: Gu Jinhua, Yang Yong

Published in 2009
by Laurence King Publishing Ltd
361–373 City Road
London ECIV ILR
Tel +44 20 7841 6900
Fax +44 20 7841 6910
E enquiries@laurenceking.com
www.laurenceking.com

All rights reserved. No part of this publication may be reproduced or transmitted in any form or by any means, electronic or mechanical, including photocopy, recording or any information storage and retrieval system, without prior permission in writing from the publisher.

A catalogue record for this book is available from the British Library

ISBN 978 185669 608 1

Printed in China

New Chinese Architecture

Zhi Wenjun Xu Jie

Laurence King Publishing

Contents

Jinhua Architecture Park, Zhejiang

Luo Xiaowei

Prologue

Rapid economic development and city expansion in contemporary China have brought numerous opportunities for architects both inside and outside China. Whether they are architects from the Chinese mainland or famous international architects, their preoccupations are about trying to find appropriate design concepts, principles and methods in such a rapidly changing environment. In the last five years, the overwhelming wave of globalization has swept every corner of the world and China has already started to catch this wave, especially with the construction of a series of projects for the 2008 Olympic Games in Beijing. At the same time, with the rapid development of the economy and the continuous improvement of living standards, exploring local methods and means of expression has become a preoccupation for more architects. Across China, the call to retain local traditions while at the same time embracing contemporary modernity is becoming more and more intense. We canonise those architects who attach importance to local requirements. They are not imitating the so-called "global standard" blindly, but manage, with great effort and perception, to retain diversity and personality in their architecture for the ultimate benefit of the people they are building for.

Times Architecture perceives the contemporary Chinese architecture with a rigorous academic spirit and critical attitude. This introduction to and explication of excellent architecture in China deserves special attention. The editorial team of Times Architecture had access to a rich accumulation of resources and laid a solid foundation for the consideration of contemporary Chinese architecture, under the leadership of Chief Editor Zhi Wenjun in particular. The editors of Times Architecture persist in carrying out site research before writing their articles in order to ensure a high standard of reportage.

Building on the work mentioned above, Times Architecture continues to lead the way for contemporary Chinese architectural publishers and select representative works with its distinctive academic sensibility and critical attitude. The 44 architectural projects included in this book, whether large or small, are of the utmost creative and critical importance in modern China, and also clearly reflect the architects' basic understanding of local history and culture as well as a smart approach to modernity. Through a detailed understanding of these architectural works, we can develop an effective means of confronting the increasingly active market. We can seek to combine local features and explore the potential of contemporary Chinese architecture.

This book aims to give prominence to technical considerations, specialities, accurate information and the time-effectiveness of a project. We hope it will benefit readers with an interest in the development of Chinese cities and their architecture.

Zhi Wenjun   Xu Jie

Reflections on the Contemporary Chinese Architecture in the Context of Globalization

Globalization is becoming an irresistible force in the context of any architecture and is gaining ever more attention. As China continues to open up to the world, the whole society is influenced by globalization to a large extent, and architecture acts as an extension of this ideology. When observing contemporary Chinese architecture, one notices that, due to China's formerly introverted, "closed door" government policy, situations such as blindly imitating Western methods without considering the local history and culture, and misinterpreting architectural concepts, arose frequently. However, as China becomes more understanding of external influences, architects are trying to find a new way of expression that balances modernity with local tradition.

Currently, Chinese architecture is gaining more recognition internationally; the quest to to perfect architectural practice is an important area of academic research. While in many Western countries the practice and theory of architecture has matured almost to the point of stagnation, the flourishing Chinese market can give imaginative architects more opportunity. With more global capital flowing into the Chinese market, the problems of how to respond to this increasingly active market and the pressures of globalization, while retaining a regional perspective, make the exploration of contemporary Chinese architecture especially interesting.

Globalization and Localization: Self-Orientation Of Chinese Architects

Globalization not only has a liberalizing tendency to break regional, racial and cultural borders, but also indicates that different racial groups will strive for the same simplified international standards – the assimilation tendency.

Cultural globalization, modernization and industrialization lead to assimilation of the global circumstance. For a developing country, it also brings the phenomenon whereby the stronger culture of the Western, developed, country dominates the weaker local culture. And just as local culture is intimidated by assimilation, regional character is at particular risk. Globalization and localization are opposing aspects of one process; they are interdependent.

With globalization and their profound national cultural roots, Chinese architects are confronted with the complex task of self-orientation. Globalization means the irresistable incursion of western architectural culture; but the decision of whether to abandon the traditional culture or not for the sake of modernity is a complex process.

Theoretically, local culture is advancing all the time with the natural development of society; but it can also be influenced by factors such as contact with external, exotic cultures. That is to say that globalization cannot take the place of localization completely, and also that localization cannot resist the globalization wave. Sometimes globalization plays the dominant role, sometimes localization does. Now, Chinese architects must find a compromise between globalization and localization in order to retain their local traditions and features, without being left behind globally.

We need to consider how to seek the balance between globalization and localization. Chinese architects always remind themselves of two issues: to keep the "localism" concept clear; and to establish an expansive, cross-cultural vision.

Western Standards and Chinese Features

The Western architectural culture has dominated the whole world for a long time, and even the globalization trend that now prevails is based on Western values.

When reviewing the development process of Chinese architecture in modern times, it is easy to find that we are in fact following the Western standards unconsciously, and even evaluating Chinese architecture with Western criteria. But undoubtedly there exists a great difference between the Western world and China, and thus we should carefully consider the social, political, economic and cultural features of our own country without blindly accepting or following the Western trend.

Chinese architects should be encouraged to think about the following questions: Do we have our own features? How should we inherit the traditional architectural culture of China? What is the Chinese character of contemporary architecture? In what ways is Chinese architecture modern? Maybe they should seek the answers both from traditional culture and the current situation of China.

With its rapid economical development, China has attracted more and more attention. In the architectural world, "Made in China" has become a hot topic. The subject has been popularised through exhibitions, architectural magazines and books published in Western countries. With the celebrations of the 2008 Olympic Games in Beijing and the 2010 World Exposition, China will become ever more prominent. This book exemplifies the process of architectural change in contemporary China, which starts from the current Chinese situation, goes through a hard practical procedure and then emerges to form its own, new, criteria.

Transverse Transplant and Longitudinal Growth

Currently, the contemporary Chinese architectural works are extending the tradition of Modernism. Their platform is Western Modernism and its value system. At present, China is at the stage of post-industrial globalization. It can only play the role of a follower in architectural theory and practice in the division of labour system. Therfore, learning from the west, or the "Transverse Transplant" phenomenon, is necessary. However, the demand of connecting with reality and our own culture – "Longitudinal Growth" – is now manifesting itself constantly in the contemporary Chinese architecture. Imitation and growth are essential in the context of all contemporary Chinese politics, economy and society. They are complementary in the multi-value system.

Universality of the Contemporary Architecture and the Current Circumstance

The starting point and main goal of the contemporary architecture is a Utopian ideal – pursuing the eternal values and universal rule of sociology and aesthetics on the basis of Rationalism; being far removed from daily life and aiming towards a pure and perfect future world. Modernist architecture is designed according to the principle of universal application. Another characteristic is efficiency-seeking. This is actualised by using industrial materials and engineering structures in the light of technical rationality, rules and procedures. It functions to serve rational people and it adopts a simple geometric form. Contemporary architecture develops in this way all around the world because of its efficiency and universality. In China, this contemporary architecture also plays an important role. It solves several problems in the progress of instant urbanization and raises the efficiency of architectural design.

However, the monotonous environment brought about by contemporary architecture and urban planning is now regarded as damaging to the urban history and culture. The loss of this Utopian ideal was a turning point in architectural theory. On one hand, practitioners of modern architecture now turn to the present for guidance. They pay attention to history and culture, especially the complexity of daily life. On the other hand, they consider techniques and aesthetics in the professional field. They insist on self-discipline and concentrate on expressing the pure and abstract space, structure, technology and aesthetics.

Chinese architects also need to change their perspective; to pay more attention to the characteristics of circumstance and to think how to deal with practical problems. It is to be rejoiced that this is now happening.

From Top to Bottom and from Bottom to Top

The contemporary architecture is designed to be universally applied, and to be as efficient as possible. This is largely achieved through the use of industrially manufactured materials, modular components and a set of rules and procedures. It is rational and simple. But such architecture eliminates endemicity, multiplicity and peculiarity. It is born of a narcissistic "from top to bottom" design doctrine.

For Chinese architects, the tasks of actualizing architecture's geographical characteristics in the context of globalization and looking for architecture with its own characteristics in local culture are very important. This is practical wisdom responding to the challenge of globalization. As a "bottom-up" processing design philosophy, territorialism reinterprets the geographic, social and cultural signification of "endemicity". Only if the Chinese architects are familiar with local culture will they be able to follow this approach successfully.

In recent years, Chinese architects have been devoting themselves to researching local culture. They adopt a bottom-up thought-processing style. The architectural style that has resulted, based on construction methods, materials and society receives wide publicity.

The Lack of the Contemporary Chinese Architecture

In the past 20 years, the development speed of Chinese society has been incredible, and yet the Chinese have not rid themselves of material scarcity and are still in the process of industrialization and urbanization. At the same time, technical expertise, economic strength and knowledge of aesthetics are all in short supply. Therefore the contemporary Chinese architecture and the planning of cities mostly follow the logic of consumption. The production of physical space and aesthetic symbols is based on the profit-maximization principle. The over-pursuit of quantity, scale and speed became the ultimate activators of Chinese large-scale, high-speed urbanization. Architecture of different types and styles flourished over a short period of time. Various urban development theories were applied all at the same time, which brought about both homogenization and fragmentation.

The purpose of doing more with less and prevalent status anxiety made the contemporary Chinese architecture tend towards dandyism, resulting in the stylization of the architectural environment.

Furthermore, the contemporary Chinese architecture cannot only connect with autologous culture and thought. It is inclined to depend on fragmentation and the transplantation of Western theories. Many of these architectural works are dissociated from reality.

All in all, the development status of China and the state of the contemporary Chinese architecture are consistent. But if China were to carry out the architectural transformation that was achieved in one hundred years in the Western World in twenty years, so much the better.

Look for Our Own Answer

The achievement of China's reform and its opening up to the outside world in the past thirty years is unprecedented. However, China is still a developing country and is confronted with many problems (the Wenchuan Earthquake in Sichuan province is a real example of such a problem), as well as the reality of huge population, weak economic foundation and imbalanced development. Therefore, plenty of academics have entreated that we must evaluate the development of China objectively by careful comprehension of the current circumstance rather than in light of the Western standard.

Chinese architects are also faced with various contradictions in such circumstances, and are trying to seek better solutions. Architectural practice and theory are becoming more complicated than at any other time due to the influences of economy, culture and so on. It is rather urgent and necessary for us to regard architecture as one branch of dominant culture and a resurgence of social ideology; in other words, as a means of cultural development. On one hand, we should study architecture with regard to social, political, economic and cultural factors; but on the other perhaps we should only study the architecture itself, for it can also be regarded as an abstract product of self-development.

At present "territorialism" is the theoretical reference for many of the questions frequently asked, such as "Where is contemporary Chinese architecture going?" or "How best to work with Chinese tradition?" In fact, territorialism is not the specific form of the architecture, but is the social circumstance.

The contemporary Chinese architecture should therefore be based on current circumstance, pay more attention to daily life and play the role of leading diversified living styles. Consumption will necessarily be the most active element in and the springing point of any architecture. The contemporary Chinese architecture can only seek its own features in the frame of international vision, cultural tradition, current circumstance and personal intelligence.

About the Architectural Works in This Book

Contemporary Chinese architecture was ignored in the Western world for almost the whole of the 20th century. As faithful followers of Western architecture, China has contributed nothing to the numerous architectural works in the world compared to Japan or India. However, in the past ten years, the major cities in China have developed very quickly, demonstrating the developing speed of China in the general context of globalization. The increasing wealth in China, together with the encroaching Western culture creates a dynamic environment for Chinese architecture that attracts designers from all over the world. A large number of architectural works have been designed which manifest the diverse development of modern and contemporary Chinese architecture.

Meanwhile, the Western world shows more and more interest in the contemporary Chinese architecture and attaches greater importance to it. Moreover, Western academics are starting to investigate the contemporary Chinese architecture – and the whole world starts to perceive China afresh.

The 44 architectural works selected in this book, no matter how large or small, are among the most creative and influential examples in China. The book provides an overview of the contemporary Chinese architecture in recent years, and provides a real, comprehensive understanding of Chinese architecture in the 21st century for the whole world. Most of the buildings were designed by young Chinese architects, while some are from international masters. They reflect the architects' understanding of history, culture and current circumstance from different perspectives. The designs are arranged chronologically, rather than by type to allow the reader more freedom of interpretation. This book is a snapshot of Chinese architectural actuality and offers a new starting point for readers.

Notes:

【1】 Zhi Wenjun, Pan Jiali. Discovery of China in the context of the western eyeshot—Comment on 《New Architecture in China》 [J] 《Times Architecture》, 2007 (02) : 143

【2】 Hua Xiahong. Melting in Conversion: Architecture in consumption culture [D] Doctoral dissertation of Tongji Unversity.

【3】 Ruan qingyue. Infirm Architecture [M]. Taibei: Garden Cities Cultural Undertaking LTD

【4】 Alexander Tzonis. Introduction of contemporary architecture Trend--Critical territorialism and particular design ideas [M] Alexander Tzonis. Liane Lefaivre. Critical territorialism: Architecture and its characteristic in the context of globalization. Beijing: China Architecture & Building Press, 2007.

【5】 Michael Hayes, Wu hongde Tr., Tongming Co. Critical architecture –Between culture and style [J]. 《Times Architecture》 2008(01): 116-121.

The Location of Contemporary Architecture in China

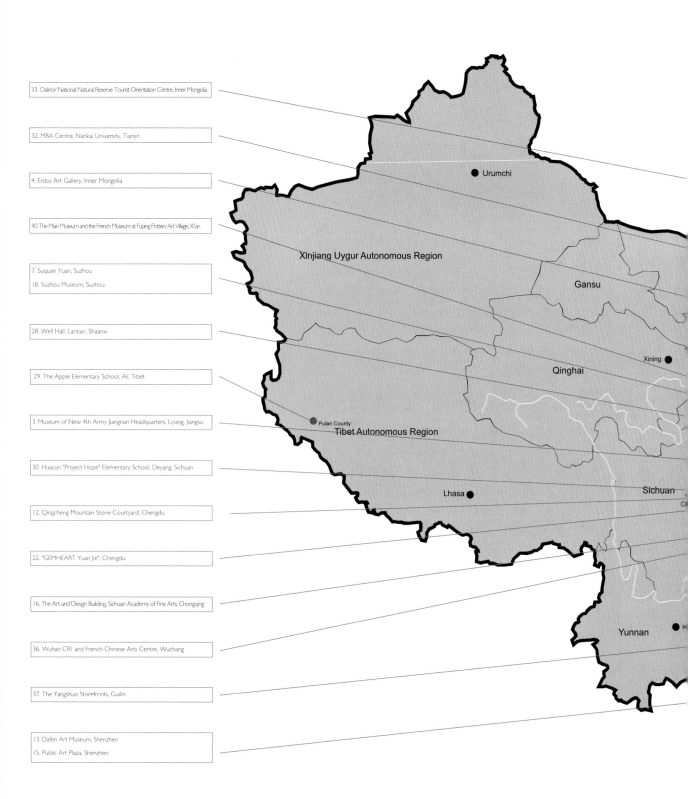

33. Dalinor National Natural Reserve Tourist Orientation Centre, Inner Mongolia

32. MBA Centre, Nankai University, Tianjin

4. Erdos Art Gallery, Inner Mongolia

40. The Main Museum and the French Museum at Fuping Pottery Art Village, Xi'an

7. Suquan Yuan, Suzhou
18. Suzhou Museum, Suzhou

28. Well Hall, Lantian, Shaanxi

29. The Apple Elementary School, Ali, Tibet

3. Museum of New 4th Army Jiangnan Headquarters, Liyang, Jiangsu

30. Huacun "Project Hope" Elementary School, Deyang, Sichuan

12. Qingcheng Mountain Stone Courtyard, Chengdu

22. "GEMHEART Yuan Jie", Chengdu

16. The Art and Design Building, Sichuan Academy of Fine Arts, Chongqing

36. Wuhan CRI and French-Chinese Arts Centre, Wuchang

37. The Yangshuo Storefronts, Guilin

13. Dafen Art Museum, Shenzhen
15. Public Art Plaza, Shenzhen

Urumchi

Xinjiang Uygur Autonomous Region

Gansu

Xining

Qinghai

Pulan County

Tibet Autonomous Region

Sichuan

Lhasa

Yunnan

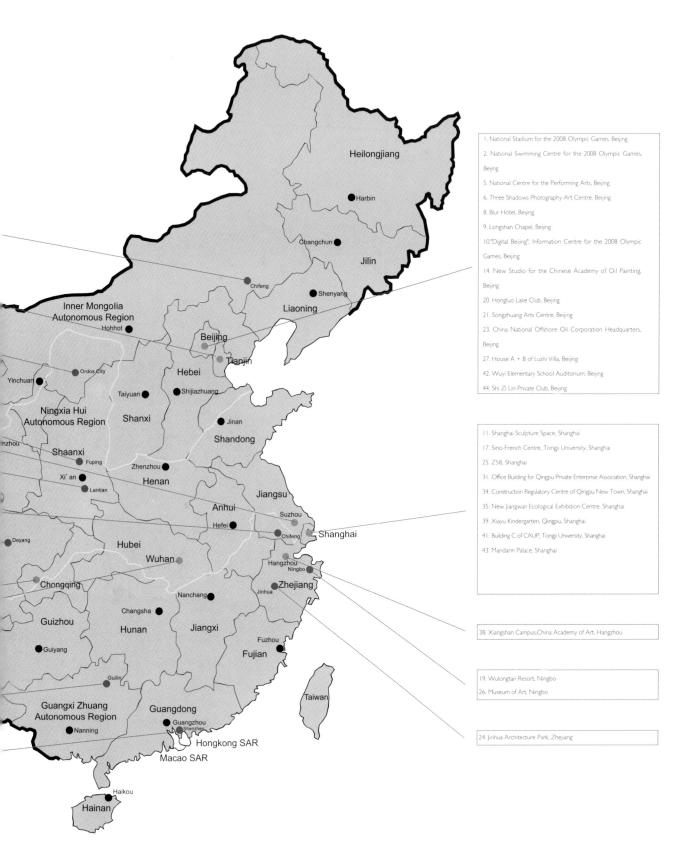

Heilongjiang

Harbin

Changchun

Jilin

Chifeng

Shenyang

Inner Mongolia
Autonomous Region

Liaoning

Hohhot

Ordos City

Beijing

Yinchuan

Tianjin

Ningxia Hui
Autonomous Region

Taiyuan

Hebei

Shijiazhuang

Shanxi

Jinan

Shandong

nzhou

Shaanxi

Fuping

Zhenzhou

Henan

Xi'an

Lantian

Jiangsu

Anhui

Suzhou

Hefei

Chifeng

Shanghai

Deyang

Hubei

Wuhan

Hangzhou
Ningbo

Chongqing

Nanchang

Zhejiang

Jinhua

Guizhou

Changsha

Hunan

Jiangxi

Guiyang

Fuzhou

Fujian

Guilin

Taiwan

Guangxi Zhuang
Autonomous Region

Guangdong

Nanning

Guangzhou

Shenzhen

Hongkong SAR

Macao SAR

Haikou

Hainan

1. National Stadium for the 2008 Olympic Games, Beijing

2. National Swimming Centre for the 2008 Olympic Games, Beijing

5. National Centre for the Performing Arts, Beijing

6. Three Shadows Photography Art Centre, Beijing

8. Blur Hotel, Beijing

9. Longshan Chapel, Beijing

10."Digital Beijing", Information Centre for the 2008 Olympic Games, Beijing

14. New Studio for the Chinese Academy of Oil Painting, Beijing

20. Hongluo Lake Club, Beijing

21. Songzhuang Arts Centre, Beijing

23. China National Offshore Oil Corporation Headquarters, Beijing

27. House A + B of Lushi Villa, Beijing

42. Wuyi Elementary School Auditorium, Beijing

44. Shi Zi Lin Private Club, Beijing

11. Shanghai Sculpture Space, Shanghai

17. Sino-French Centre, Tongji University, Shanghai

25. Z58, Shanghai

31. Office Building for Qingpu Private Enterprise Association, Shanghai

34. Construction Regulatory Centre of Qingpu New Town, Shanghai

35. New Jiangwan Ecological Exhibition Centre, Shanghai

39. Xiayu Kindergarten, Qingpu, Shanghai

41. Building C of CAUP, Tongji University, Shanghai

43. Mandarin Palace, Shanghai

38. Xiangshan Campus,China Academy of Art, Hangzhou

19. Wulongtan Resort, Ningbo

26. Museum of Art, Ningbo

24. Jinhua Architecture Park, Zhejiang

National Stadium for the 2008 Olympic Games, Beijing

Architects: Herzog & de Meuron (Switzerland); Li Xinggang (China)

Location: Beijing Olympic Park

Design / Completion: 2003.01-2005.06 / 2008.04

Area: 258,000 sqm

Architects: Herzog & de Meuron Architecture Office,
Switzerland; China Architecture Design & Research Group;
ARUP

Client: National Stadium Corporation Ltd.

The National Stadium of China is located in the south of the Olympic Green central area. It is to the east of the 200-metre wide pedestrian green space on the central axis, west of the dragon-shaped water system, south of the Zhongyi Road and north of the Nanyi Road.

The stadium is built on a sloping plinth, via which spectators can enter the stadium from the Olympic Green. To the south of the platform is the sunken warm-up area, which is connected with the main field in the stadium by the players' tunnel. The complex annex facilities and commercial outlets are arranged underground, which provides more reasonable access for different crowds and keeps the stadium itself clean and integrated. The main body of the National Stadium is an elliptical structure, 333 metres long and 69 metres tall from north to south; 294 metres wide and 40 metres tall from east to west. Its central opening is 182 metres long from north to south and 124 metres wide from east to west. The main steel structure, a colossal large-span grid formation just like a bird's nest, and the stand, a concrete bowl structure, are separated from each other. The roof is covered by a double-layer membrane structure, with a transparent ETFE membrane fixed on the upper part of the roofing structure and a translucent PTFE membrane fixed on its lower part. A PTFE acoustic ceiling is attached to the side walls of the inner ring. The spacious grid encircles the capacious concourse, which runs full-circle around the stand and functions as an open urban space with restaurants, VIP reception area and lounge. The seating bowl, like a classical arena, is divided into three tiers: upper, middle and lower. Between the upper and the middle tiers of the stand, there are the VIP box area (including 168 boxes) and VIP seats. The whole seating area can be easily accessed from the corresponding concourse.

As the main stadium of the Beijing 2008 Olympic Games, the National Stadium's seating capacity amounts to 91,000, including 11,000 temporary seats. The venue will host the opening and closing ceremonies of the Beijing Olympic Games and Paralympic Games, the

1. Overview of the
National Stadium of China

track and field competitions and the football finals. After the Olympic Games, the National Stadium will be able to accommodate 80,000 spectators. It is designed to hold special sports games, general sports games and non-sporting events (such as entertainment shows, large group events and commercial shows). As a top-class sporting venue, the main body of the National Stadium has a design life of 100 years.

The design concepts of the National Stadium include: games and games-watching, structure–form integration and landscape–building integration. Meanwhile, new technologies, new materials and new methodologies are applied to the project, such as large-span grid formation; highly sophisticated design; manufacturing, processing and installation of the bending-torsional steel components; design and construction of the double-layer membrane structure; the highly integrated roof rainwater drainage system; computer simulation-based fire strategy; thermal and ventilation amenities, and acoustic environment; Green Olympics projects (such as utilization of rain and flood, geothermal heat pump and solar energy); and CATIA-based three-dimensional design.

(All pictures supplied by project architects. Photographers: Zhang Guangyuan, Li Xingguang)

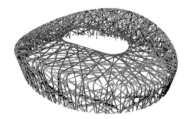
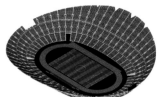

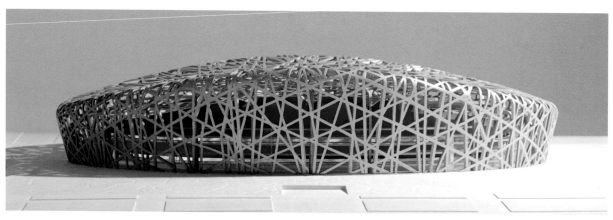

2

3

2. The generation of the design
3. Model
4. Partial view

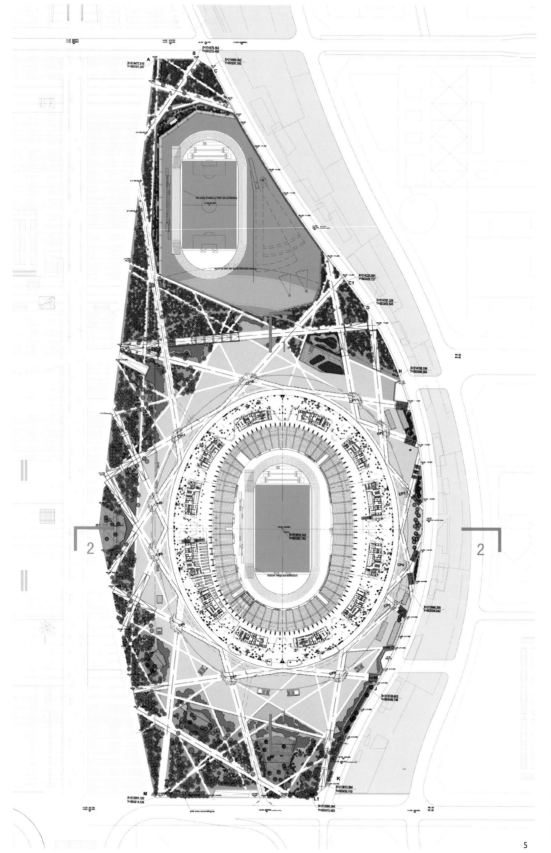

5. Site plan

6. Panoramic view of the stadium field

7. 8. Sections

5

6

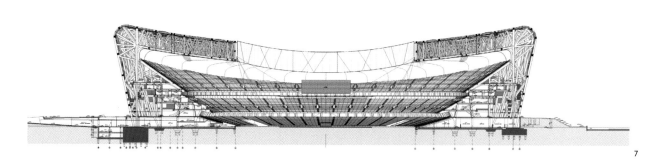

7

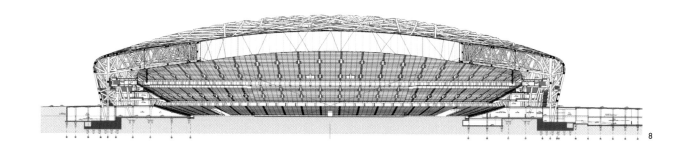

8

9. Grand staircase
10. Night view
11. Night view of main entrance

National Swimming Centre for the 2008 Olympic Games, Beijing

Architects: PTW, CCDI, ARUP

Location: Beijing Olympic Park
Design / Completion: 2003 / 2008
Area: 87,000 sqm
Architects: PTW Architects; CSCEC; CCDI Design; Arup - John Bilmon, Mark Butler, Chris Bosse, Zhao Xiaojun, Zheng Fang, Wang Min, Shang Hong, Tristram Carfrae, Peter Macdonald, Kenneth Ma, Haico Schepers
Client: Beijing State-owned Assets Management Co., Ltd

The National Swimming Centre (NSC) was central to the success of the 2008 Olympic Games, with all the pools and functions that FINA needed to conduct every session of swimming, diving, water polo and even synchronised swimming. NSC is also a truly multi-functional leisure centre for Beijing in the 21st century. It encapsulates every aspect of water – hot and cold, shallow and deep, lazy rivers and pounding surf beaches, competition pools... and even has ice.

From the planning stage of the Olympic Park, the National Swimming Centre was designed to support the National Stadium – the "Bird's Nest", designed by Herzog & de Meuron. NSC demonstrates its wisdom and beauty without a big gesture that competes with or overpowers the National Stadium. As a counterpoint to the exciting, energy-giving, masculine, totemic image of the National Stadium, the "Water Cube" appears as serene, emotion-engaging, ethereal and poetic; evoking feelings associated with water.

The design process of the National Swimming Centre involved a concerted collaboration of international teams. Architects from PTW helped a lot with the skin material, Ethylene Tetra Fluoro Ethylene (ETFE); engineers from ARUP developed a perfect structural model based on foam theory; and the design group from CCDI gave the idea of the "Water Cube" and endowed it with meanings from Chinese traditional philosophy. The design collaboration itself was a joyful journey, which inosculated the different ways of art, culture and technique, as well as the 2008 Olympic Games in Beijing.

The architects use the idea of water not only as a decorative feature but also by exploring the very molecular structure of water in its foam state. This forms the façade's structural system and gives the "Water Cube" its appearance. The molecular structure softens the building's edges and faces.

The façade system comprises a series of panelled units that are mounted as internal and external skins, made up of a series of ETFE bubbles.

1. The "Water Cube" in winter

The structure of the National Swimming Centre is based on the most efficient subdivision of three-dimensional space. It is derived from Kelvin's "foam theory", which is a geometry problem: "If we try and subdivide three-dimensional space into multiple compartments, each of equal volume, what shape would they be when the subdividing surfaces are of minimum area?"

This is an interesting problem, not only as a theoretical exercise, but also because such shapes are prevalent in nature. The study of soap shows that when soap films come together, they always meet as three surfaces coming together at 120 degrees to form at edge. And these edges always meet, four to a corner, at the tetrahedral angle of approximately 109.47 degrees.

Despite its apparent complexity and organic form, the NSC is in fact based on a high degree of repetition. It uses only three different faces, four different edges and three different corners or nodes. So the Beijing NSC was easily and efficiently constructed making use of a highly repetitive, organic space-frame based on a solution to one of the world's greatest mathematical challenges which is also common throughout nature – resulting in a social, technical and green solution.

(All pictures supplied by project architects.)

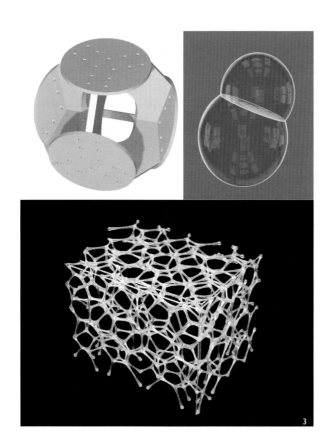

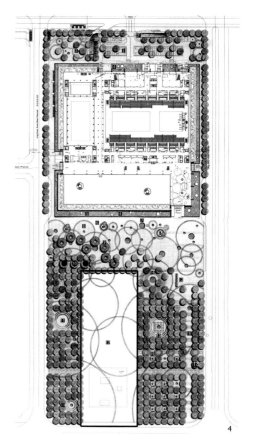

2. Reflective effect of ETFE bubbles at dusk

3. Weaire-Phela computer model

4. Siteplan of the "Water Cube"

5. Exterior view of the "Water Cube"

6

6. View of roof

7. Undergroud floor plan

8. Seating plan

9. East elevation

10. Section of Olympics mode

11. Section after Olympics

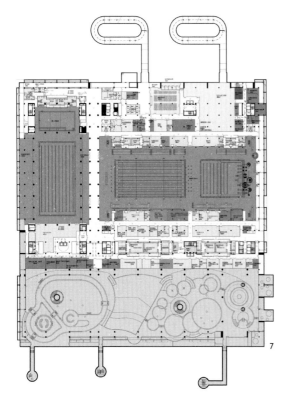

7

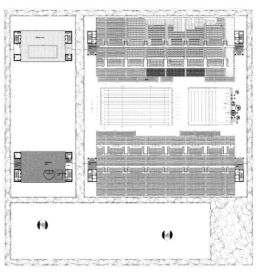

8

9

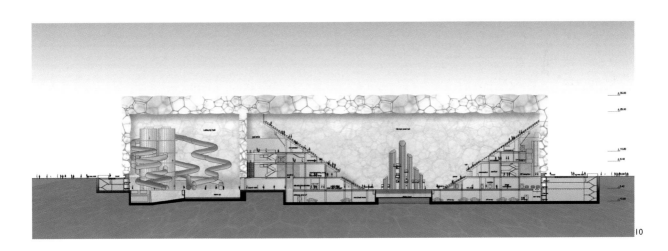

10

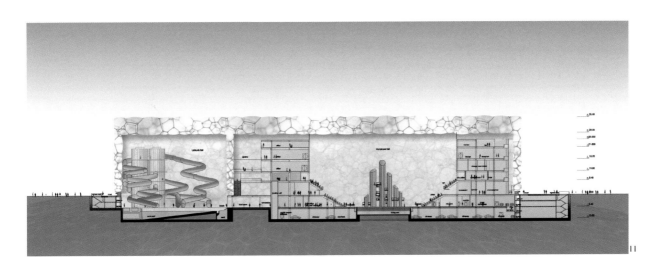

11

12. Main lobby
13. Interior view
14. Competition hall

13

14

Museum of New 4th Army Jiangnan Headquarters, Liyang, Jiangsu

Architect: Zhang Lei

Location: Shuixi Village, Liyang, Jiangsu

Design / Completion: 2006.03 / 2007.12

Area: 3,000 sqm

Architects: Zhang Lei; Shen Kaikang / AZL Atelier Zhanglei

Client: Liyang Cultural Bureau

The Museum of New 4th Army Jiangnan Headquarters is located in Shuixi village, Liyang, 70 km to the southeast of Nanjing. It has unusual and important historic significance to Liyang, a town with a population of 300,000. In this location, the New 4th Army battled uphill against the Japanese invasion near Liyang in the 1930s and 1940s. The Liyang municipal government has now attempted to make the museum an education centre in revolutionary tradition for young people.

This memorial attempts to be:

1) A landmark building; a memorial for the city that commemorates the historic people and events of the Chinese revolution; 2) A symbolic building, which reminds people of the uphill battles years before; 3) A localised building, which has unique local colour and features; 4) A usable building, which can meet the requirements of exhibiting historical data.

Since ancient times, rocks and stones have been used to commemorate people and events. A geometrical body of rock with deep and irregular cracks lies across the field, facing the historical site of the New 4th Army Jiangnan Headquarters. This expression seems deceptively simple but also retains rich metaphorical potential.

Against the background of the surrounding golden cornfields, the museum appears as a vast rock monument lying on the ground. The regular geometrical body rises from the horizon as a huge mass, heightening its memorial meaning and sense of power.

Vivid red incisions are made on the surface of the rock, which allude to the bloodiness of the war and the unyielding battle. Though embedded in the deep-grey exterior wall, the red cuts seem to emerge from the background.

The incisions make holes in the plane, which show up as different functions and forms in the interior space. They interrupt the geometry of the plane and bring vertical scale to the interior space of the museum, implying the courtyards common in local traditional architecture.

(All pictures supplied by project architects.)

1. Exterior view

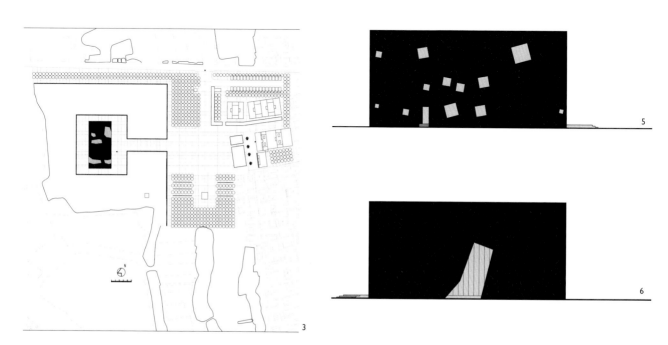

2. Exterior view from the south
3. Site plan
4. Exterior view from the west

5. 6. 7. 8. Elevations

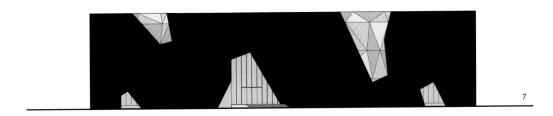

7

8

9. Entrance to the square

10. Distant view

11. Ground floor plan

12. 1st floor plan

13. 14. 15. Sections

16. View from the courtyard

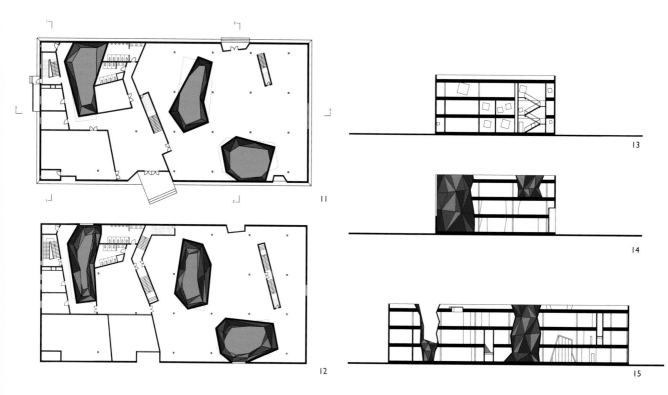

Erdos Art Gallery, Inner Mongolia

Architect: Xu Tiantian

Location: Kokoshina Cultural District, Erdos
Design / Completion: 2006.02 / 2007.08
Area: 2,700 sqm
Architects: Xu Tiantian, Guillaume, Chen Yingnan
Client: Jiang Yuan Water Conservancy Construction Co. Ltd., Erdos

The natural environment of the wild prairie in Erdos is an opportunity for – or perhaps a challenge to – architects. It is purely natural and is hardly possible to meet with. As the launch project of the overall development of the district, the gallery appears to be the first step in blending new architectural works into the landscape.

As can be seen from the project's concept map, there is no design, no label, no image; not even any symbolic meanings. What the architect has done is to simply trace a tortuous route through the wild land and put it inside a box. Although the route is a little bit convoluted, the unadorned skin gives clarity to the architecture, and becomes the outstanding feature of the project.

Inside the gallery, the exhibition is shown by a linear route: through the low horizontal entrance, zig-zagging along the natural terrain of the dune's slope, going up, and then turning back to the ground-floor exhibition hall regarded not only as the end of the public exhibition, but also marking the start of the private research area. The exit faces the entrance, which means that the traffic inside the building follows a double-loop route. The structure winds along the dune, forming semi-enclosed courtyards or squares by interacting with the terrain. This linear space is continuous, forming cross-sections that vary in size, height and width according to the terrain. Landscapes, spaces and terrain are blended with each other in various ways: overlooking the reservoir through the glazed wall; introducing the landscape of courtyards into the interior space through the continuous glazing of the side walls; enclosing the exhibits below roof lights. As a result, the interior lighting is varied as well. Light and shadow are interlaced in the space, in which the artworks in the interior and the natural landscape on the exterior unfold gradually into one another. This makes for a pleasant experience for visitors, who move freely between experiencing the artworks, the building itself and the natural landscape.

(All pictures supplied by project architects.)

1. Exterior view

2. Distant view

3. Site plan

4. Rendered computer model

5. 6. Path / circulation

3

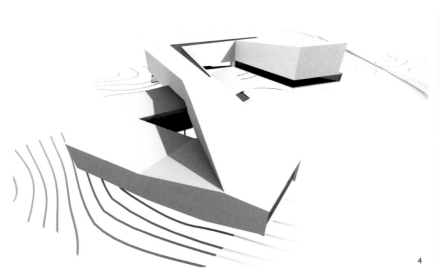

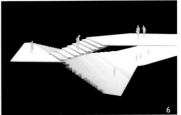

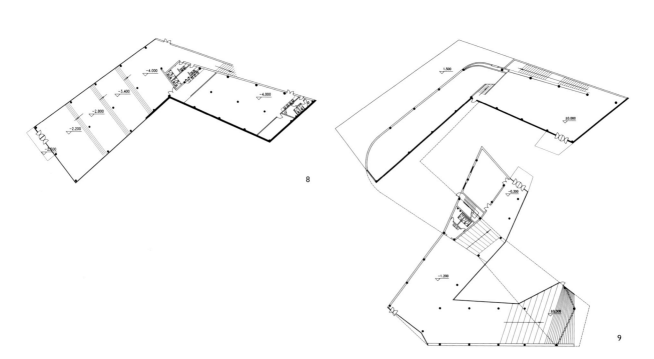

8

9

10

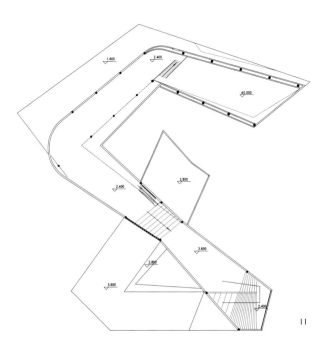

11

7. Exterior view
8. Basement plan
9. Ground floor plan
10. Entrance
11. 1st floor plan

12. Courtyard

13. Circulation diagram

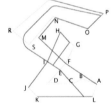

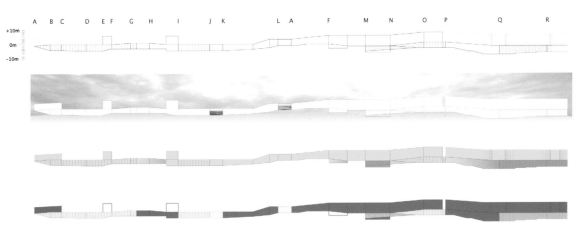

14

15

14. 15. Interior
views
16. Courtyard

17. 18. Interior
views

National Centre for the Performing Arts, Beijing

Architect: Paul Andreu (France)

Location: Beijing
Design / Completion: 1999 / 2007
Area: 172,800 sqm
Architects: Paul Andreu Architects, Paris — (Paul Andreu (Principal),
    François Tamisier, Serge Carillion, Olivia Faury, Mario Flory, Herve Langlais
Project architects: Aeroports de Paris Ingenierie,
    Beijing Institute of Architecture & Design
Consultants: Centre Technique et Scientifique du Batiment (acoustical)
Client: Client's Committee of National Centre for the Performing Arts

1. Exterior view
2. Site plan

The National Centre for the Performing Arts (NCPA) complex houses a 2,500-seat opera house, a 2,000-seat concert hall, a 1,200-seat drama hall and a 300–500-seat multi-functional theatre. With the improvement of cultural life in China, there is a demand for better performing arts venues. People are no longer satisfied with a single, multi-purpose space for all kinds of performances. The NCPA, as a complex for performing arts which comprises different special theatres that can accommodate various performances to best effect, embodies the burgeoning cultural life of the country as well as the region.

The proscenium arch of the opera house is 18.6 metres wide. As a national opera house, the size of its proscenium arch is larger than the regional ones, allowing for greater scope in set design. The opera house has a seating capacity of 2,500, which includes the seats in the pit and the last three rows of standing places behind the seats on the first floor. This arrangement provides excellent audio and visual effects, as well as enough seats.

After a period of adjustment and amendment, the layout is now able to meet the usage requirements. For example, the complicated circulation and logistics are arranged systematically and run smoothly. The subway station to the north is connected with the NCPA by tunnels, through which many people can enter the centre directly from the subway station. In addition, parking areas for vehicles and bicycles are both situated on the basement level. Spectators can enter the centre directly from the parking area through the entrance, seven metres underground. All the passages are underwater; one of the main features of the layout. Going through the underwater passages, spectators are led to an impressive grand hall over 40 metres high. The entry for stage properties is at the south gate underground, to keep the ground floor clear and uncluttered. The main entrance faces the west side of the Great Hall of the People (GHP), thus minimizing the disturbance to the GHP.

The roof of the NCPA, together with its steel structure, internal

ceiling and skin, cost 350 million RMB. It would have cost more if a glazed curtain wall had been applied. Some have criticized the egg-shaped structure, saying that it is too big, resulting in wasted space and energy. In fact, the volume of the overground part is 790,000 cubic metres, and the total volume is 1,330,000 cubic metres including the underground part; relatively small when compared with other, similar structures.

Fire protection has been fully taken into account in the design. Besides the common facilities for fire alarm, fire extinguishing and fire diffusion prevention, the flow of people during evacuation has been taken account of in the design of the structure. When the fire alarm is activated, all occupants can be evacuated to the safe area within five minutes. There have been concerns that, if the pool were to be damaged by an earthquake or terrorist act, the water would flood into the underground parts of the buildings with disastrous results. To solve this problem, the pool is divided into 22 units by walls 10 cm

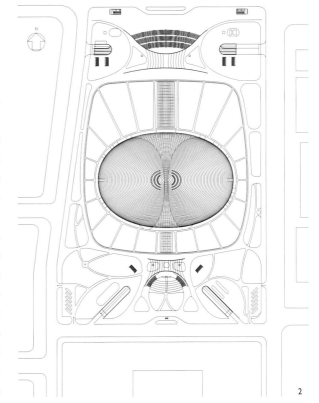

under the surface. If any damage were to occur, only the top 10 cm of water and the water in one unit – about 4,000 cubic metres of water in total – would leak into the basement to a height of only 20 cm, and be unlikely to cause injury or loss of life.

(All pictures supplied by project architects. Photographers: Fu Xing, Paul Maurer)

3

3. Panoramic view

4. Exterior view
5. Basement plan
6. Night view of lobby
7. 8. Sections

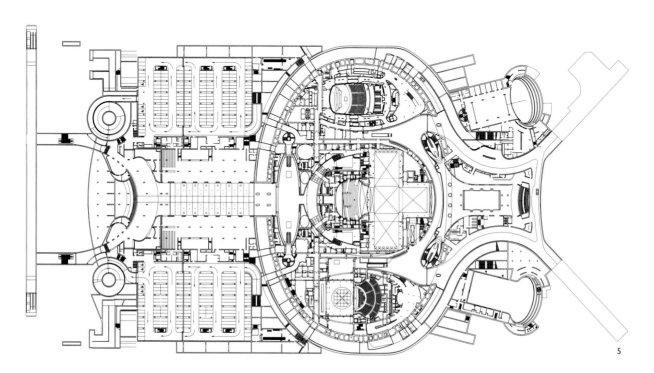

5

6

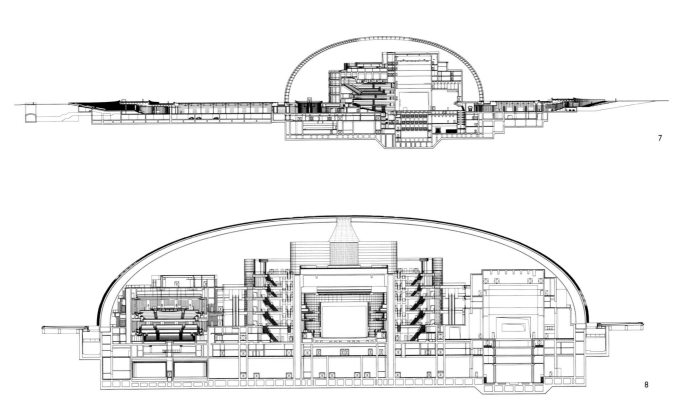

7

8

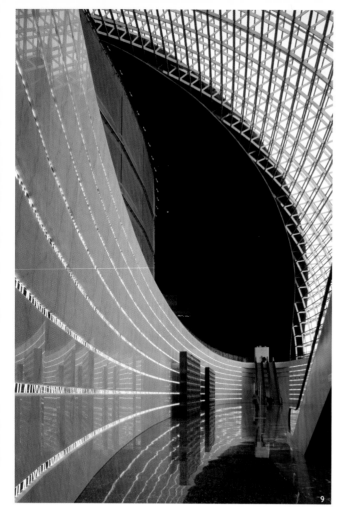

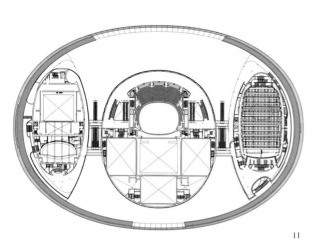

11

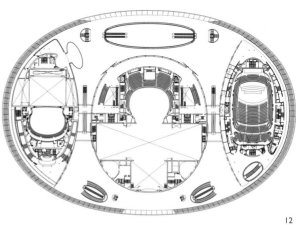

12

9.10. Interior views

11. 2nd floor plan

12. Ground floor plan

13. Lobby

14

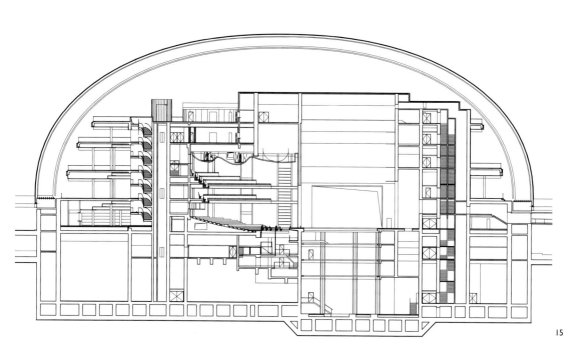

15

14.16.17. Opera hall

15. Section of opera hall

18

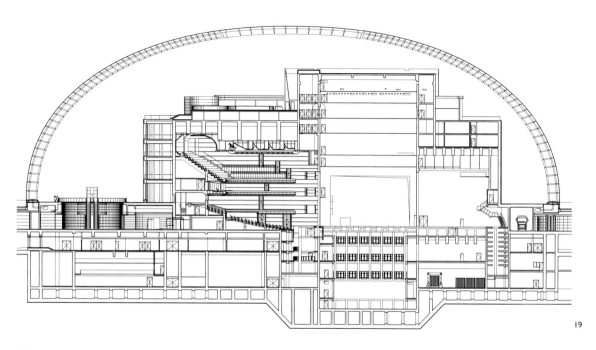

19

18. Auditorium of theatre
19. Section of theatre
20. Auditorium of concert hall
21. Section of concert hall

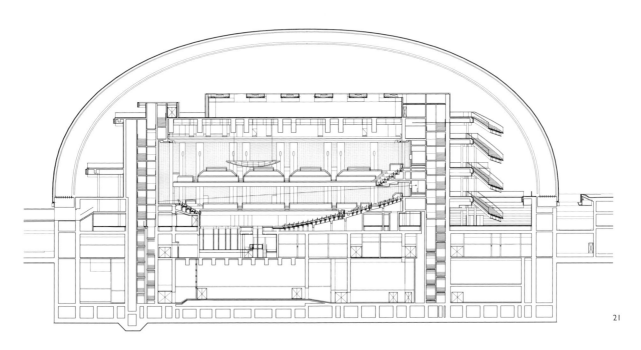

21

Three Shadows Photographic Arts Centre, Beijing

Achitect: Ai Weiwei

Location: 155 Caochangdi, Chaoyang District, Beijing,
Design / Completion: 2006.07 / 2007.06
Area: 2,600 sqm
Achitects: FAKE Design - Ai Weiwei, Andy Lee, Conner
Wingfield, Hash, Mike, Vesna, Sun Zhipeng
Client: RongRong & inri

Just beyond the fifth ring road, within the boundaries of Cao Chang Di, lies a burgeoning community of artists and galleries contributing to the development of contemporary Chinese art.

Situated in the northern fringes of the village, adjacent to CAAW (China Art and Archives), exists the site of an abandoned factory, an automobile repair shop and a storefront which were leased in combination to give a total area of 4,600 square metres.

By redefining the functionality and use of the "factory" model, new relationships were created to bridge the gap between the production and the consumption of an image, creating a multi-functional platform for photographic exhibitions, including processing and developing studios, administrative offices, archives, a café and a library.

(All pictures supplied by project architects.)

1. Courtyard
2. Facade detail

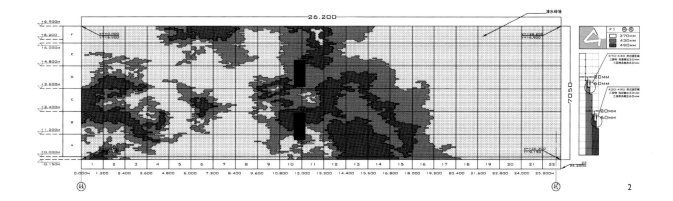

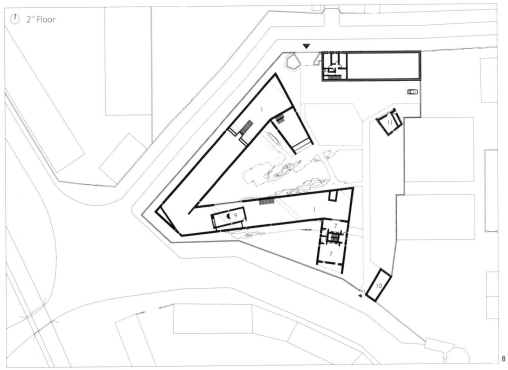

2nd Floor

1 Exhibition   2 Darkroom   3 Drying chamber   4 Storeroom   5 Café   6 Kitchen   7 Bedroom
8 Duplicating   9 Management   10 Boiler   11 Power distribution   12 Courtyard

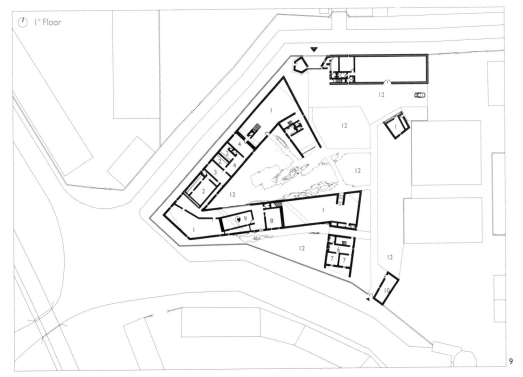

1st Floor

3. Courtyard
4. 5. 6. 7. Sections
8. 1st floor plan
9. Ground floor plan

11. Interior view of main exhibition hall

Suquan Yuan, Suzhou

Architect: Tong Ming

Location: 711, Shiquan Road, Suzhou

Design: 2004.05 / 2006.07

Area: 5,613 sqm

Architect: Tong Ming

Client: Zhongcheng Real Estate Development, Suzhou

1. Entrance

Suquan Yuan is a redevelopment project which was planned to turn a huge parking space previously reserved for a tourism company into shopping and resort areas.

There were two challenging aspects to this project: one was the bottle-necked entrance which is only six metres wide in contrast to the spacious compound inside. Although it was quite appropriate previously for safeguarding and managing reasons, it is relatively disadvantageous for a commercial space to be segregated from the street front in this way.

The other point was the uncertainty of the usage of the project. Like most speculative developments, it is impossible to have a final user or definite functional purposes for the buildings in mind during the design and construction process. Therefore, an adaptable spatial strategy is more important than a definite function proposition.

When considering the problem of identity for a project, an impressive building must be better than a billboard, and a lively scene must be better than a static image. The entrance club itself should be an impressive sign that

conveys instant information about what is happening inside the compound.

Based on the impressions and memories of local traditional architecture, the entrance club, which is supposed to be a coffee shop, was designed as a dark-brick box inserted into a wooden box, whose long windows can be opened or closed according to the internal conditions. The façade of the building is an indicator and projects images of different situations. The material and pattern of the windows generate a pure box of light and shadows.

In order to provide a flexible space for the future users, a standard and easy structure independent from function was decided on, following Le Corbusier's DOM-INO diagram. The spaces inside were distinguished as served area and servant rooms. The served area is a pure geometric space that will receive light and shadows from the windows; the servant rooms occupy the residual spaces between the main room and site boundary.

The club building was also designed as a reaction to the street and the plane trees on the west and south. The building is a box that could

72

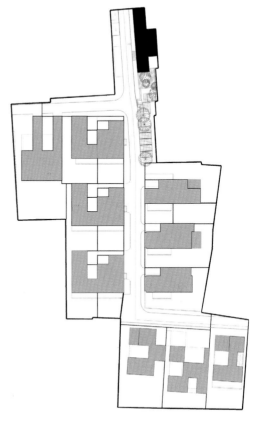

2. South view of the cafe

3. Site plan

3

accommodate uncertain further users, who would sit on different floors and have their respective views over the street and the trees. The club itself is a stage that anticipates inhabitation by future events.

(All pictures supplied by project architect. Photographer: Lü Hengzhong)

75

4. Partial view of west facade
5. Northwest view at night

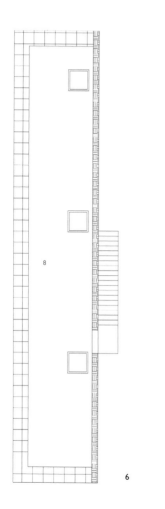

6

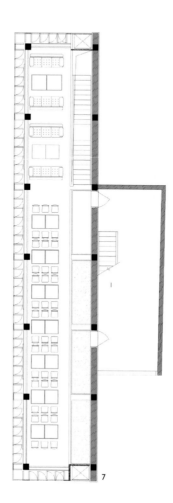

7

1 Outdoor area   5 Kitchen   8 Flat roof
2 Outdoor walkway 6 Storeroom   9 Pond
3 Cafe   7 Toilets
4 Bar

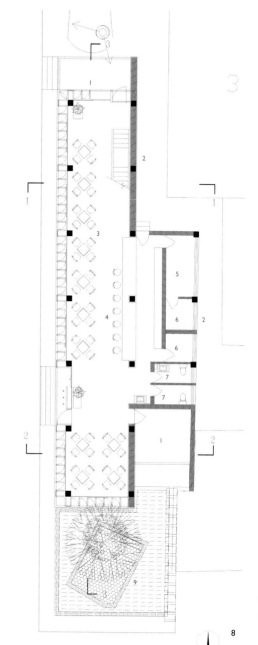

8

6. Roof plan

7. 1st floor plan

8. Ground floor plan

9. Interior view of the ground floor

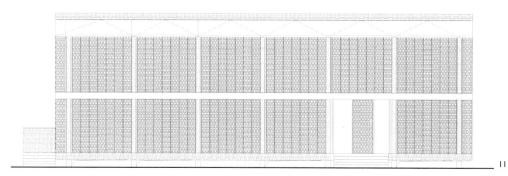

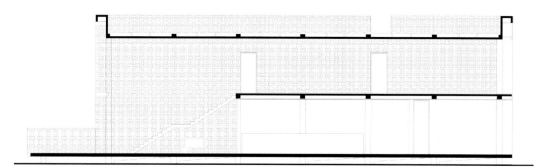

10. Interior view of the ground floor
11. West facade
12. Section
13. Interior view of the 1st floor
14. South facade
15. North facade

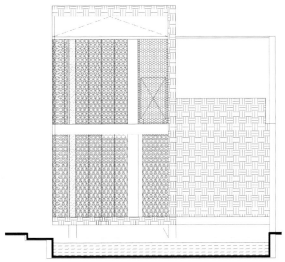

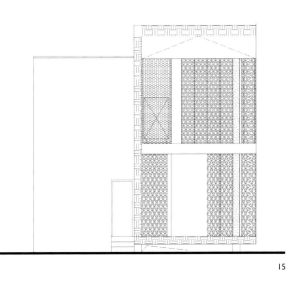

16.17. Details of lattice on facade

18. 19. Sections

20. Terrace on the 1st floor

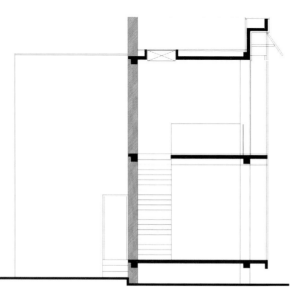

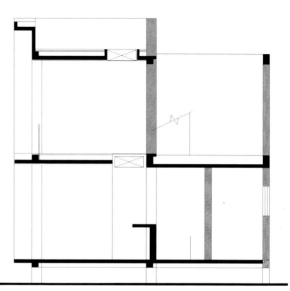

18

19

Blur Hotel, Beijing

Architect: Zhu Pei

Location: Beijing, China

Design / Completion: 2005 / 2006

Building Area: 10,176 sqm

Architects: Zhu Pei, Wu Tong, Li Chun, Zhang Pengpeng, Zhou Lijun, Dai Lili, Wang Min

Client: China Resource

Beijing was once one of the best-preserved medieval cities in the world. Since 1949, however, the location of government and industrial premises within the centre of the city has disrupted the once free-flowing and hierarchical city plan with the construction of enclosed, large-scale buildings placed with no regard to the rhythm and consistency of the old city. The development of these "tumours" within the ancient Ming dynasty core has resulted in the creation of a disjointed and incomprehensible city centre.

In response to this problem, Blur Hotel, located on the site of a large government office beside the Western Gate of the Forbidden City, is an experiment in "urban acupuncture". Rather than operate and remove the tumour (in other words demolish yet again), a far less disruptive and harmful method is to leave it in place and simply neutralise its ill effects. As a refurbishment proposal, the project aims to harmonize the existing building with its surroundings without resorting to backward-looking pastiche, and provide a beacon for renewal of the surrounding area.

The first strategy employed with this end in mind is to open out the ground floor of the building to create a layer of traversable space occupied by public-oriented programmes. The next approach aims to integrate the building more with the local building typology of the sihueyuan, or courtyard house. By simply carving into the concrete slab floors of the existing building, an arrangement of alternating vertical courtyards is created, replicating the spatial arrangement of the surrounding hutongs. With the interior of the building transformed, the third and final tactic deals with the exterior of the building, wrapping it in a continuous and semi-transparent façade. Referring to local traditions, this skin is based on the image of a Chinese lantern. Allowing light out of and into the building on every floor, it diffuses the building into a single, but permeable, object.

(All pictures supplied by project architects.)

1. Facade detail

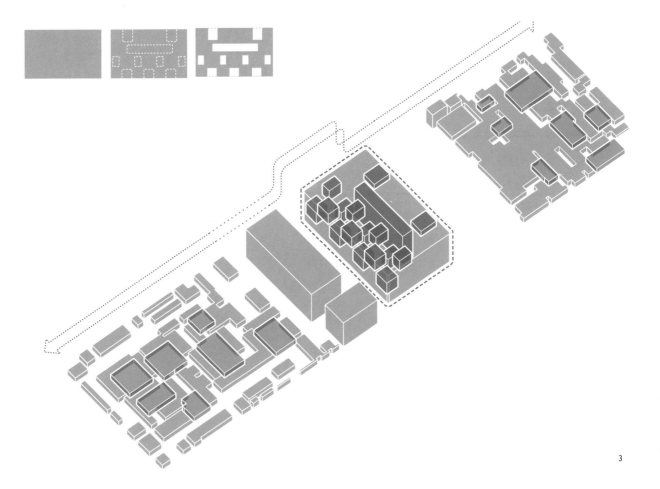

3

2. Exterior view

3. Vertical courtyards

4. Site plan

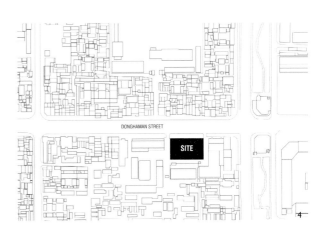

DONGHAMAN STREET

SITE

4

WEST ELEVATION

0 1m   5m   10m

5

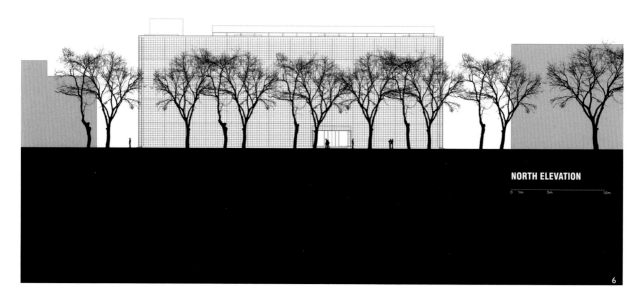

NORTH ELEVATION

0 1m   5m   10m

6

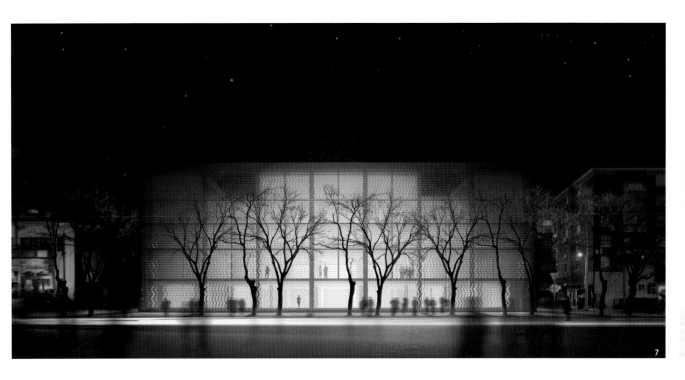

5. West elevation
6. North elevation
7. Night view
8. Model

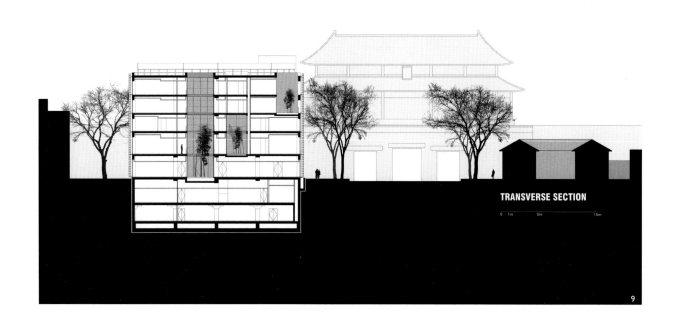

TRANSVERSE SECTION

0 1m   5m   10m

9

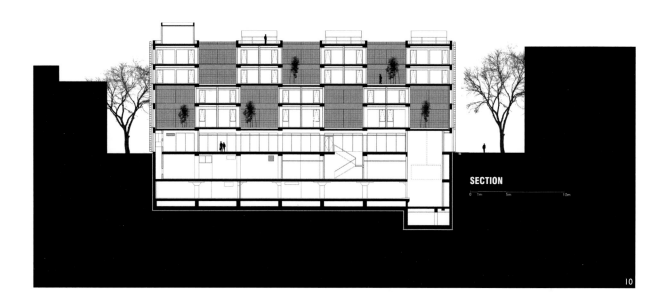

SECTION

0 1m   5m   10m

10

9. 10. Sections

11. Courtyard

12.13. Facade detail

Longshan Chapel, Beijing

Architect: WSP

Location: Huairou district, Beijing

Completion: 2007

Area: 1,300 sqm

Architect: Zhang Ying

Client: Xinxin Town

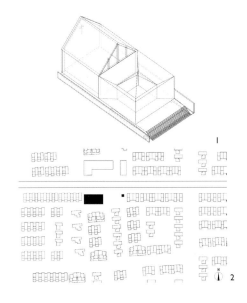

Thanks to the original intention to build a cultural place, the Longshan chapel was born from the "Town Masterplanning" of Xinxin town in the Huairou district of Beijing. The Longshan chapel impresses viewers with its plain temperament, compact geometrical structure and clear, functional layout. Its concept is based on analysis of the current plot and surrounding buildings: within the limited land area, the main building and belfry are separated from each other, at either end of the plot. Between them, an open space almost the same size as the chapel body is formed, like a square, to extend the area for public activities. Located at the intersection of main roads, the 30-metre high belfry becomes the central landmark of the town. The main building rises gradually from the steps to the lobby and then the main hall. With a sloping roof structure, the 18-metre high main hall corresponds with the sloping-roofed houses nearby. As a result, looking from the southern residential path, the main building seems to disappear, but the tall and graceful belfry stands upright and

peaceful under the blue sky.

In the main building, the "material spaces" such as the facilities room and operating room, are in the basement, while on the ground floor, the lobby and main hall, as "spiritual spaces", consist of two linked square spaces. These two kinds of space: one is concave and another is protruding; one is modest and another is showy; form a sharp contrast in the structuring of the space.

The design and construction of Longshan Chapel used modular systems, which made the processes more rational and systematic. The main building is placed alongside the southern residential path, and its north end aligns with the buildings in the eastern residential area. It forms a 16.8 m × 33.6 m rectangle, using 4.2 m modular units. The main hall and the lobby take 4 × 4 units, and the colonnade in the lobby takes 2 × 2 units. The heights of the façades of the main hall and lobby are four units and two units respectively, while the 1 × 1 units used for the exterior face of the belfry also fit the spiral

1. Form of main building
2. Site plan
3. Northwest view

staircase. However, the control of the modules has not been strictly executed. Column grid spacing is 4.2 m in the vertical axis, but 4 m in the horizontal axis, because the modular grid is not fixed on the central axis of the exterior wall, but is measured from the basalt curtain wall.

In the lobby, surfaces and columns are all clad in warm-coloured sandstone. In the main hall, the plasterboard ceiling is set below the concrete girders. The interior spaces are stuccoed with white paint, and lit evenly by sliding windows. The design not only continues the purity of the exterior spaces, but also forms a sharp contrast in the brightness and temperature of the colours used. Moreover, there are gaps at the intersections of wall and floor slab, column and ceiling, column and floor; which not only clarifies the structural logic of different components of the building, but also enhances the control over the long-term quality of the building, by avoiding the splits caused when

different materials expand an contract at different temperatures.

(All pictures supplied by project architects.)

5

6

4. Interior view of the corridor

5. Model

6. Interior view of the hall

7. 1st floor plan

8. Ground floor plan

9. Basement plan

10. Analytical drawing of main building

11. Modular grid of the ground floor

1 Atrium
2 Corridor

7

1 Main lobby
2 Front lobby
3 Storeroom
4 Pond
5 Ramp
6 Bell tower

8

1 Office building
2 Machine room

9

10

grid modulus: 4. 2m×4. 2m

11

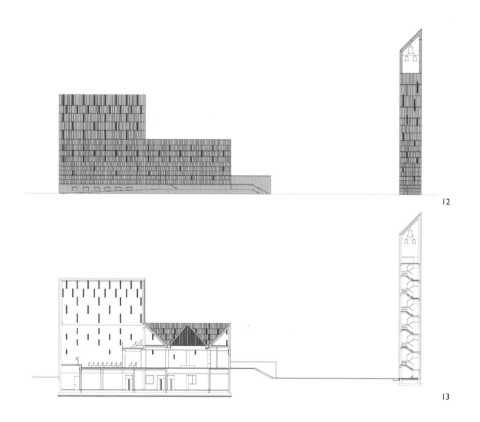

12

13

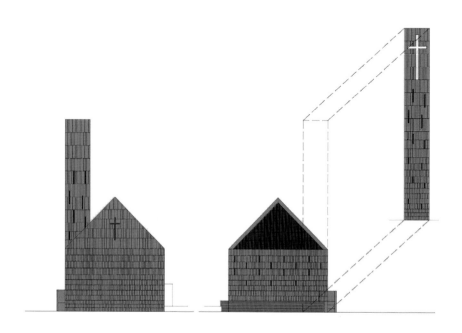

14

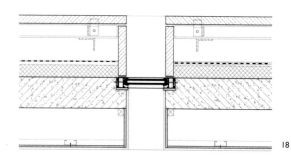

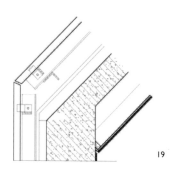

16. 17. Interior views of the main hall

18. Basalt curtain wall and window detail

19. The ceiling of the main hall

20. Night view

"Digital Beijing", Information Centre for the 2008 Olympic Games, Beijing

Architect: Zhu Pei

Location: Beijing Olympic Park, Beijing

Design / Completion: 2004-2005 / 2006-2007

Area: 98,000 sqm

Architects: Zhu Pei, Wu Tong, Wang Hui, Liu Wentian, Li Chun,

Lin Lin, Tian Qi

Client: Beijing Network Information Industry Office

The Beijing Municipal Government promised the world that Beijing would present an Olympics with the highest technological content in history in 2008. As the landmark building of the "Digital Olympics", the Digital Beijing Building is located at the northern end of the central axis, neighbouring the core area of the Olympics Centre, the National Stadium and the National Swimming Centre. Seven internationally renowned architectural firms participated in the competition for "Digital Beijing".

The Digital Beijing Building, nearly 100,000 square metres in area, served as the control centre and the data centre of the Beijing Olympics. Afterwards, it will accommodate a virtual museum of the Digital Olympics and an exhibition centre for manufacturers of digital products.

The rapid development of the digital age has greatly impacted on Chinese society and its cities. If the industrial revolution resulted in Modernism, the Digital Beijing Building begins to explore what will occur in the digital epoch.

The concept for Digital Beijing was developed through reconsideration of and reflection on contemporary architecture in the era of digital information. Appearing like a digital barcode, or an integrated circuitboard, it emerges from a serene water surface. It resembles a specific form; revealing an enlarged micro-world suggestive of the microchips abundant but ignored in our daily life. With an abstracted mass, like the simple repetition of the digits 0 and 1, this building will be an impressive symbol of the Digital Olympics and of the information era.

In the future, we expect the Digital Beijing Building will always be under renovation, evolving and keeping pace with technology.

(Pictures supplied by project architects. Photographer: Marc Gerritsen, Fang Zhengning.)

1. South facade
2. Site plan

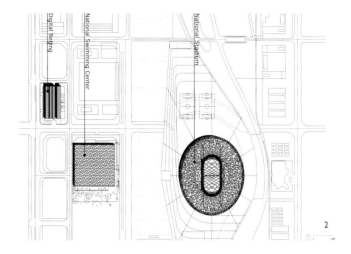

3. Southwest view
4. East view
5. East elevation
6. West elevation

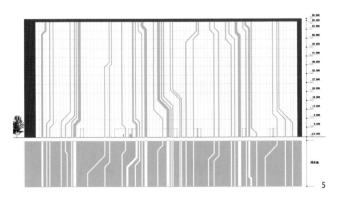

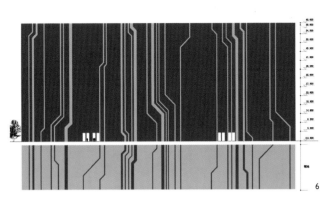

7. View of bridge

8. 2nd floor plan

9. 3rd floor plan

10. Ground floor
plan

11. 1st floor plan

12. Night view

7

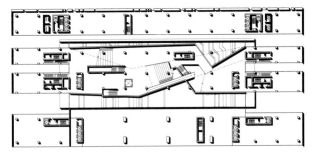

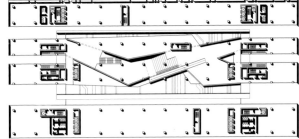

2nd Level ⌐ ⌐ 8

3rd Level ⌐ ⌐ 9

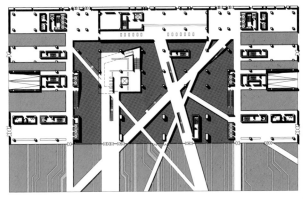

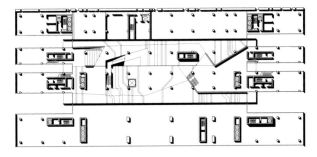

Ground Level ⌐ 10

1st Level ⌐ ⌐ 11

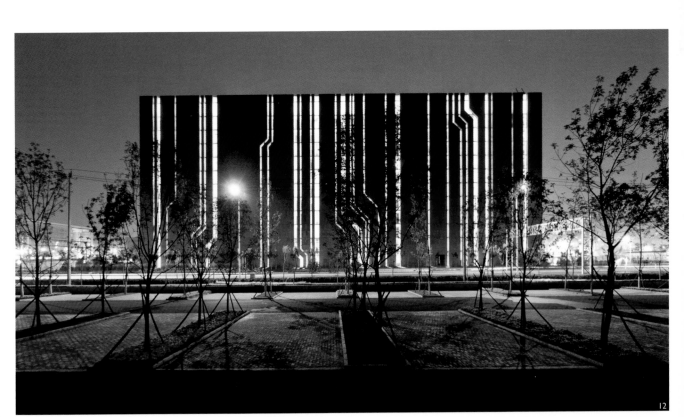

12

13

14

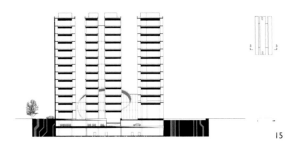

15

13.14.17. Interior views

15. 16. Sections

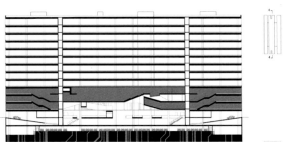

16

Shanghai Sculpture Space, Shanghai

Architect: W & R Group, Deshaus, BAU, Qingdao Times Design

Location: 570, West Huaihai Road, Shanghai

Function: Culture and art community centre

Site area: 55,000 sqm

Gross area: 46,000 sqm (phase I: 20,000 sqm, phase II: 26,000 sqm)

Block A, Phase I: 2,500 sqm, for art exhibition;

Block B, Phase I: 8,900 sqm, for art exhibition, offices for creative industry, etc;

Block C, Phase I: 6,600 sqm, for offices and supporting facilities of creative industry, etc;

Block D, Phase II: 5,150 sqm, for cultural offices;

Block E, Phase II: 4,600 sqm, for cultural offices;

Block F, Phase II: 6,400 sqm, for art exhibitions and supporting facilities, etc;

Block G, Phase II: 8,400 sqm, for art exhibitions, offices and supporting facilities for creative industry, etc;

Block 3, Phase II: 10,540 sqm, for art exhibitions and offices of creative industry;

Block H, Phase III: 2,000 sqm, for art exhibitions and supporting facilities, etc.

Architects: W&R Group, Deshaus, BAU, Qingdao Times Design

In early 2005, the Office of Shanghai Urban Sculpture Committee and the Board of Shanghai Urban Planning Administration, together with other social organizations, with reference to the successful international practice of building public arts centres out of old deserted factory workshop buildings, chose a deserted steel-plant workshop located at 570 West Huaihai Road (the former No. 10 Steel Plant of Shanghai Steel Company) as the site for Shanghai Sculpture Space. By protective renovation and the remoulding of its functions, the old workshop was regenerated to become a public arts centre, which not only embodies the vigour of urban art and the spirit of modern times, but also inherits the urban historical legacy.

The project, comprising two phases, covers an area of about 56,000 square metres, with a total construction area of about 45,000 square metres. The first phase, with a floor area of about 20,000 square metres, includes sections A, B, C and H, and building No. 1; the second phase, with a floor area of about 26,000 square metres, includes sections D, E, F and G and building No. 3. The construction is based on the principle

of "controlling the overall scale, respecting the historical structure of the old buildings, keeping the historical features of the industrial buildings, and promoting the interactions between the new and the old buildings".

Sections A, B and C of the first phase and section F of the second phase used to be the main building of the cold-rolled band steel workshop and the acid-cleaning workshop of the former No. 10 Steel Plant of Shanghai Steel Company. The former buildings are well kept, so the reconstruction is consistent with the principle of "rebuilding the old as the old". The truss structure, the high and spacious space and the sunken space have been preserved as much as possible, and have been reinforced appropriately. The exterior wall has been cleaned and reinforced, which highlights the former texture and preserves the style of the former architecture. After reconstruction, section A becomes an exhibition space, while sections C, B and F become ideal venues for artistic display, original works and support facilities.

As for sections D, E and G of the second phase, the former buildings

1. Partial view of exhibition hall entrance

were not well kept and are smaller in scale, so they are reconstructed with expansions that are absolutely independent from the old buildings. The new and the old are linked by connecting structures, which integrates the buildings as a whole with functions as exhibition space and offices. Each building unit is provided with a public space, which makes it possible to embrace multi-functional uses.

Section H and building No. 3 are newly completed. In order to keep the spaciousness of the central space and foster an easy and relaxed atmosphere, section H is an earth-sheltered structure, which creates a good relationship between the building and the environment, and is in harmony with the old buildings. Building No. 3 is situated south of the central green space. Its cast in-situ concrete structure is consistent with the red brick/grey wall style of the other buildings.

From the point of view of the architectural design, almost all the lower floors are higher than 5.4 metres, and quite a lot of the spaces of the former buildings are fully preserved, which ensures the multi-functional nature of the space. As for the landscape design, the former crane beams in the deserted site become seats in the new environment; the weight cast with "Shanghai Metallurgical Bureau" in Chinese characters becomes a sculpture; and the stone pickling bath is put in the central green space.

(All pictures supplied by project architects.)

2. Exhibition hall entrance

3. Interior view of exhibition hall

4. Site plan

5. Model

6. 7. 8. 9. Sections

☐	Extended construction
▨	Rebuilt construction

1   Building No.1
2   Block A
3   Block B
4   Block C
5   Block D
6   Block E
7   Block F
8   Block G
9   Block H
10 Building No.3

4

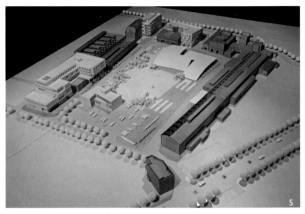

5

3

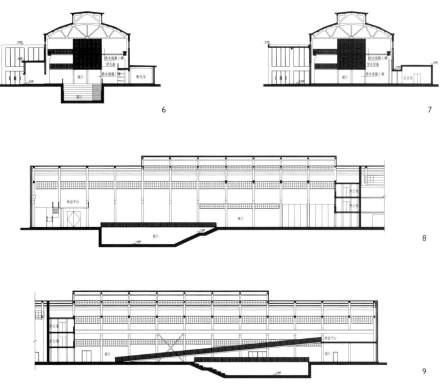

6

7

8

9

10

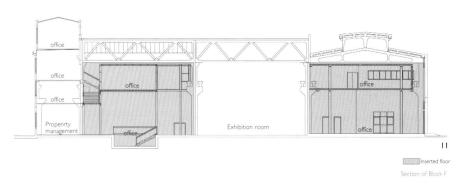

11

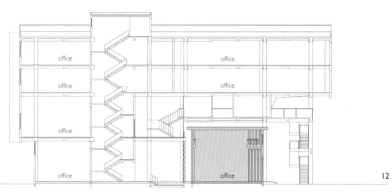

12

Inserted floor

Section of Block F

Original building

Section of Block G

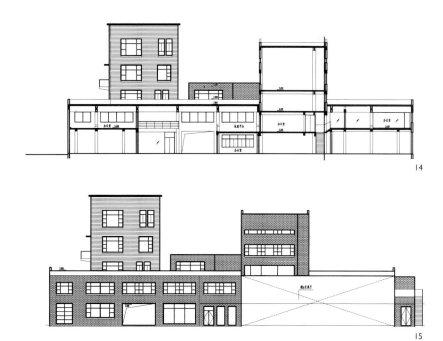

10. Outside

11. Section of Block F

12. Section of Block G

13. Exterior view of phase III, Block H

14.15. Sections

Qingcheng Mountain Stone Courtyard, Chengdu

Architect: Standard Architecture

Location: Qingcheng Mountain, Daguan Town, Chengdu, Sichuan

Design / Completion: 2005 / 2007

Area: 480 sqm

Architects: Zhang Ke, Zhang Hong, Wang Andong, Liu Yabo, Wang Tong, Hao Zengrui, Carla Maria Freitas Goncalves, Liu Xinjie, Yang Xinrong, Zhang Zhengfan

Client: Sichuan Jinlian Corporation

1. Entrance

The "Stone Courtyard" Tea House is located close to Daguan Town at the foot of the Qingcheng Mountain near Chengdu. With a total area of 500 square metres, the tea house actually comprises five separate courtyard buildings standing very close to each other. The first building is an empty front courtyard; the last building functions as living courtyards; and the other three buildings function as tea courtyards.

Local craftsmen were involved in the design and construction of the wooden roof structure. Looking from the interior, the wooden roof would have appeared completely traditional if the columns near the patio had not been carefully removed.

The stone wall is built exclusively of a type of local slate, which will be covered by green moss in a few years after being exposed to the rainy and humid weather of Chengdu.

(All pictures supplied by project architects. Photographer: Chen Shuo)

1

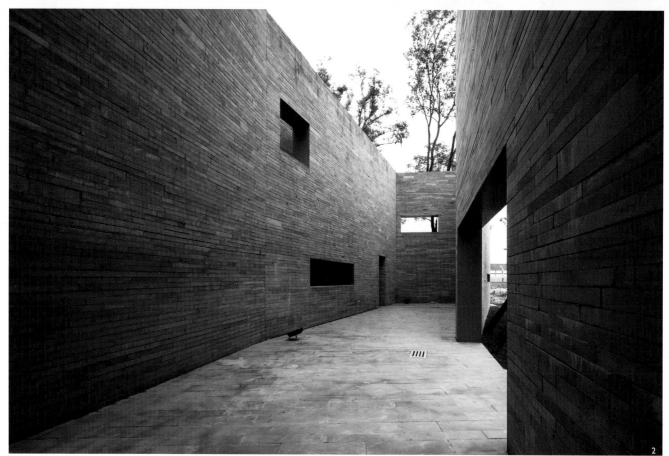

2. The entrance to the tea courtyards

3. Model

4. Roof plan

5. Ground floor plan

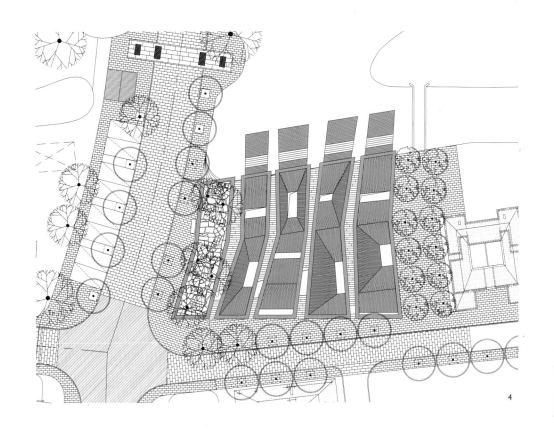

4

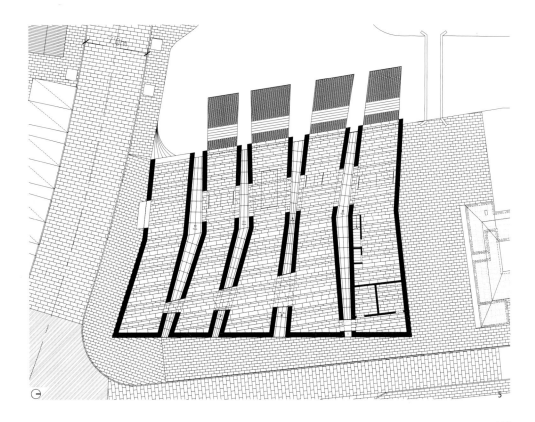

5

6. The empty courtyard viewed from an opening

7. Section of tea courtyard B

8. The small alley between the empty courtyard and the tea courtyard

9. Section of tea courtyard A

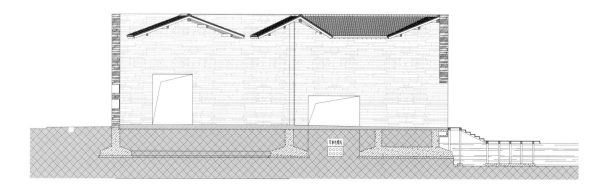

8

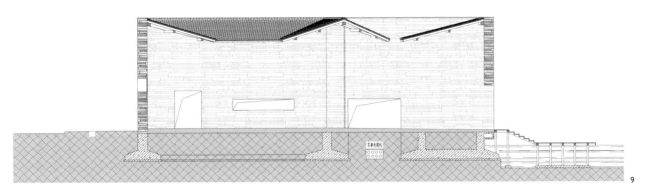

9

10. The main entrance of the stone courtyard from the southwest

11. South facade of the stone courtyard

12. West view

13. Facade of the small alley

14. East facade

12

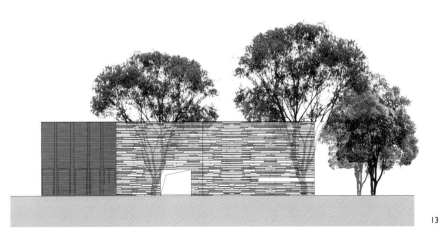

13

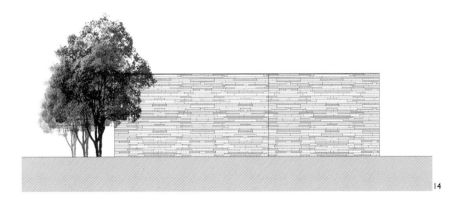

14

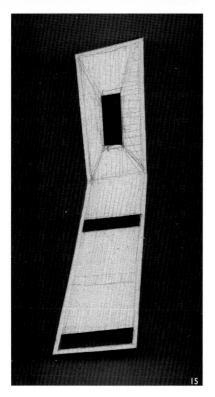

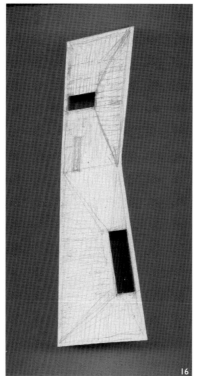

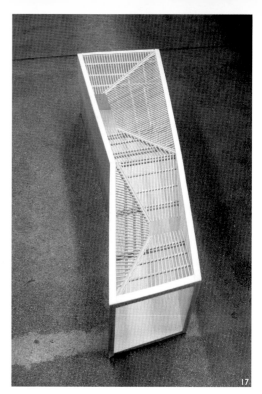

15. Model of tea courtyard B

16. Model of tea courtyard C

17. Model of the roof structure

18. Wooden structure of the roof

19. Interior of tea courtyard C

Dafen Art Museum, Shenzhen

Architect: URBANUS

Location: Dafen Village, Shenzhen
Design / Completion: 2005-2006 / 2007
Area: 17,000 sqm
Architect: URBANUS
Client: Dafen Village

1. Overview of the
site
2. Site plan

Dafen village is in Buji Township, Longgang District, Shenzhen. Best known for its replica oil painting workshops and manufacturers, its exports to Asia, Europe and America bring in billions of RMB each year to the area.

The concept focuses on reinterpreting the urban and cultural implications of Dafen Village, which has long been considered as a strange mix of pop art, bad taste, and commercialism. A typical art museum would be considered out of place in the context of Dafen's peculiar urban culture. The question is whether or not it can be a breeding ground for contemporary art and take on the more challenging role of blending with the surrounding urban fabric in terms of spatial connections, art activities and everyday life. Therefore the strategy was to create a hybridized mix of different programmes, like art museums, oil painting galleries and shops, commercial spaces, rental workshops and studios under one roof. It also creates maximum interaction among people by creating several pathways through the building's public spaces. The museum is sandwiched by commercial and other public programmes which intentionally allow for visual and spatial interactions among different functions. Exhibition, trade, painting and residence can happen simultaneously, and can be interwoven into a whole new urban mechanism.

(All pictures supplied by project architect. Photographer: Chen Jiu)

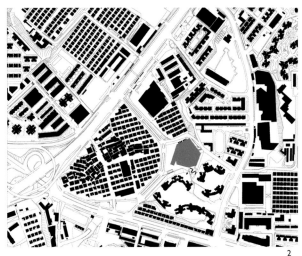

3

3. Overview of the museum

4. Overview of main entrance

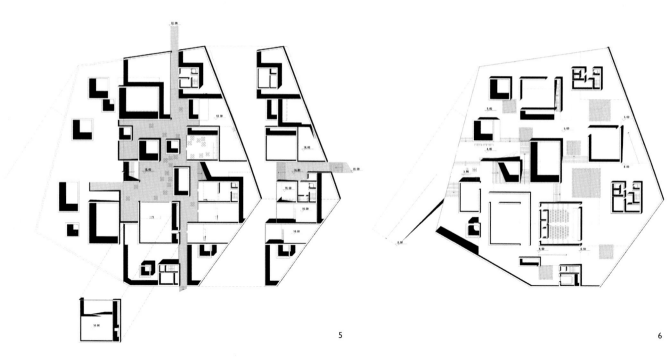

5

6

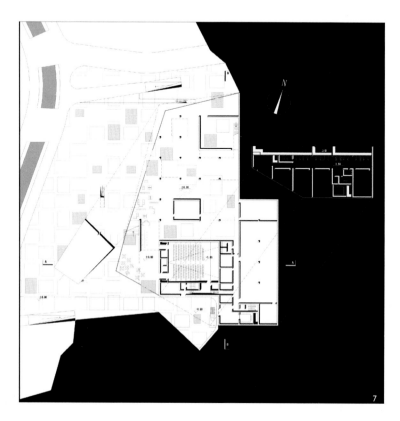

7

5. Ground floor plan

6. 1st floor plan

7. Basement plan

8. Staircase

9. Exhibition hall
10. Patio analysis
11. Leaning interior wall

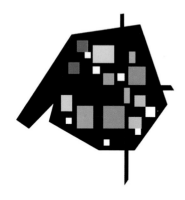
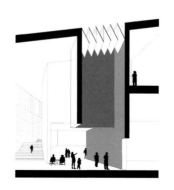
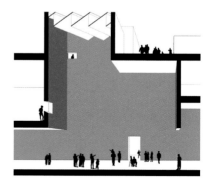
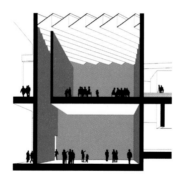
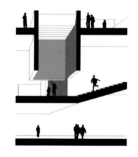

10

12. Exterior wall detail
13. Exterior wall detail on roof plaza
14.15. Design concept of facade
16.17. Design concept of site

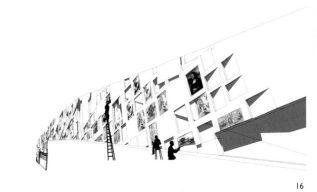

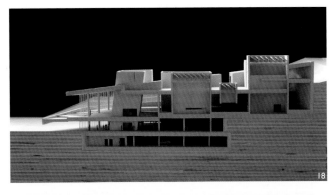

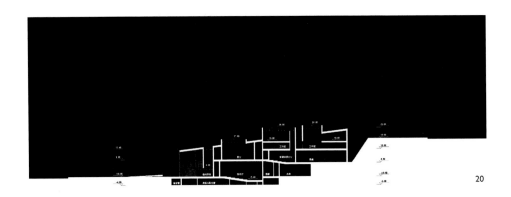

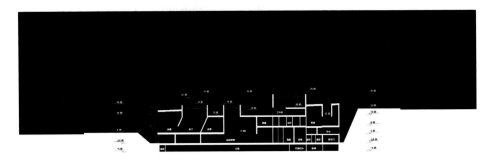

New Studio for Chinese Academy of Oil Painting, Beijing

Architect: Han Tao

Location: Beijing

Design / Completion: 2005-2006 / 2006-2007

Area: 1,400 sqm

Architect: Han Tao

Client: Mr Yang Feiyun, Chinese Academy of Oil Painting

The studio is tailored to classical oil paintings created by the artists of the Chinese Academy of Oil Painting, headed by Mr Yang Yunfei. The artists require a studio suitable for sketching and painting, with enough space in which to create painting series and large-scale paintings.

Research was carried out into the lighting, size and scale of the studio space. To some extent, the artists' needs are inter-related. The light in the studio should be non-uniform and diversified in colour temperature and lighting levels. As for size and scale, these depend on the size and scale of the works being created.

By analyzing studio spaces and interviewing artists, it was found that the light in the studio should be north daylight, rather than south sunlight. The lights are classified by angles of incidence as top light, high sidelight or sidelight. Top light should not be cast into the centre of the room, for that will result in too much uniform light in the interior. Instead, it should be cast on the northern part of the

room, resulting in light and shade. The skylights should be arranged 70–80 degrees northward. By this means, sunlight will penetrate into the interior space only at noon in summer, while the rest of the time, stable daylight can be diffused into the interior space, ensuring brightness even when it is cloudy. If the skylights are set 45–65 degrees northward, although direct sunlight can be diffused by opaque glass, the incoming light is of poorer quality. By setting a north window higher than 4 metres and through the use of adjustable curtains or blinds, sidelight and high sidelight can be brought into the interior space; drawing the curtains over the lower part of the window will result in high sidelight, while drawing the curtains over the upper part of the window will result in sidelight. The windowsill should be set up 0.45 metres above the ground – a classical height that allows artists good light to work on figure paintings. Different artists have different requirements governing the distance between the window and the side wall. For example, the window in Jan

1. East view of new studio and existing building

Vermeer's studio was close to the side wall. However, most artists require about a one-metre distance between the window and side wall, in order to be able to place props obscured in the shadow behind the model. In addition, by modifying the sloping angle of the roof, the reflection intensity in the interior space can be adjusted. (If the space is high enough, this sloping angle is not necessary.)

Features of the wall body and the roof structure include the wall, with two 240-mm thick layers and a 50-mm thick stressed plastic sheet in the middle for thermal insulation. The wall is 550 mm thick in total, which makes all the structural columns and ring beams punch out of the façade. The beams are concealed, so the large-scale interior space appears to be entirely composed of wall panels, and the brick–concrete structure is simplified. The texture of the interior wall surface is made of white cement mixed with sand in the proportion of 1:3 and coated with plaster, which forms a warm and light tone of grey that is suitable as a background for painting. For the same reason, the brick wall pattern shows at irregular intervals, which is contrary to the principle of minimalism that is currently fashionable in architecture.

(All pictures supplied by project architects. Photographer: An Li, Duan Meng)

2. Pond between new studio and existing building

4

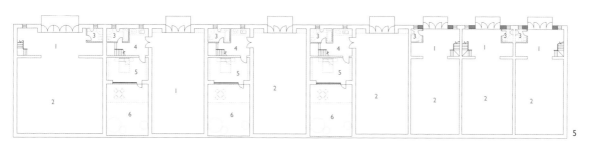

5

1 Entrance lobby   4 Storeroom   7 Small studio
2 Large studio   5 Bedroom   8 Large studio atrium
3 Toilets   6 Outdoor area   9 Gazebo

6

The process of study on sections of studio space structure

798

Segment of a typical unit → Adjusting the roof inclination and the spatial depth → Opening the north wall a. Big studio

Bedroom from a residential building from the Renaissance period

Segment of a typical unit → Adjusting the roof inclination and increasing the intensity of light reflection → Opening the south b. Small studio wall

a+b+c: Typical section of the studio area

Bedroom from a modern residential building

Section of a typical unit/recess for the entrance area

Opening the south wall

Service area

Section of a typical unit/ increasing the south high windows

Typical modern art exhibition space

Section of a typical unit/stretching towards the south courtyard

Typical modern living room/bedroom

m+n: Typical section of the living area

Typical modern factory

Soviet-style factory

Grand public hall from the neo-classical period

Post-modernist exhibition hall

Oil painting studio in the China Academy of Art

Church/palace from the Renaissance period

A
16X7.8m
158 m2

Size and proportion of A-type studio

Sectional space structure of A-type studio

C
16X13.2m
260 m2

Size and proportion of C-type studio

Sectional space structure of C-type studio

B
16X14.7m
220 m2

Size and proportion of B-type studio

Sectional space structure of B-type studio

Sectional space structure of the living area of B-type studio

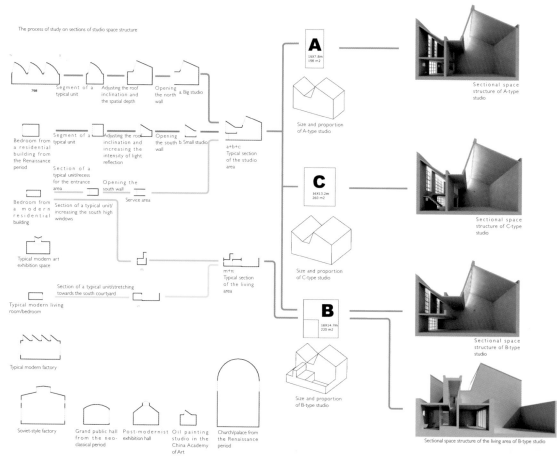

1 Large studio
2 Small studio
3 Bedroom
4 Outdoor area
5 Gazebo

7. Studio C, small atelier on 1st floor
8. Study of light, new studio
9.10. Studio C, grand atelier and small ateliers
11.12. Sections
13. Studio B, view of grand atelier

14

14. Studio C, view of small atelier from grand atelier

15.16. Study of light, small atelier of Studio C

17. Study of light, Studio B

18

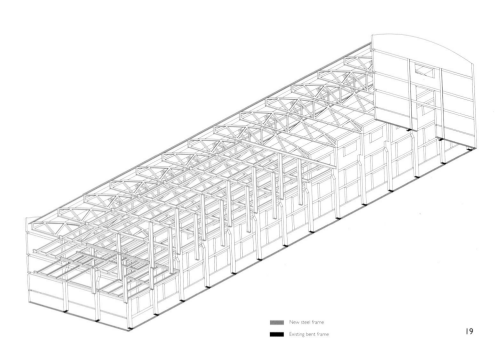

New steel frame
Existing bent frame

19

20

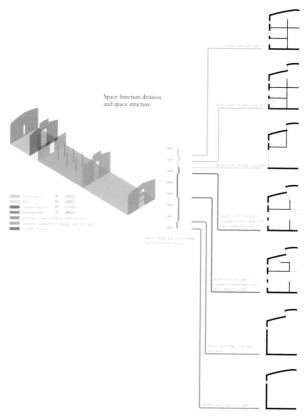

Space function division
and space structure

18. West view of grand exhibition space, ground floor

19. Diagram of existing bent frame and new steel frame

20. View of grand exhibition space from central glass corridor on the 1st floor

21. Renovation analysis

21

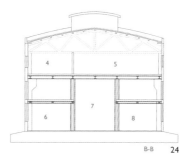

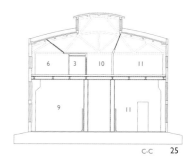

1 Reading room	6 Bedroom	11 Studio
2 Doorway	7 Reception hall	
3 Toilets	8 Kitchen	
4 Study room	9 Teaching area	
5 Large studio	10 Air corridor	

A-A **23**

B-B **24**

C-C **25**

22. View of small ateliers from central glass corridor

23. 24. 25. Sections

26.27. Plan of the renovation of the existing building

1 Showroom	5 Kitchen	room	10 Showroom atrium	13 Reading room	16 Private studio
2 Teaching area	6 Utility room	8 Conference waiting	11 Studios	14 Air corridor	17 Private study
3 Doorway	7 Assembly	room	12 Bedrooms	15 Doorway	18 Private bedroom
4 Dining room		9 Bedroom			

Public Art Plaza, Shenzhen

Architect: URBANUS

Location: Luohu District, Shenzhen

Design / Completion: 2000 / 2007

Area: 5,000 sqm

Architects: Meng Yan, Liu Xiaodu

Client: Luohu Bureau of Construction Works

1. Site plan
2. Overview

Located in one of the most densely populated areas of downtown Shenzhen, the Public Art Plaza is a programme initiated by both the city administrator and the architect. Under the programme, this once-shabby parking lot will be converted into a semi-underground parking garage integrated with arts programmes such as an outdoor display area, gallery, bookshop, café, artists' studio and lecture hall.

The whole complex is composed of an elongated gallery along the north border of the site, a sloped parking garage in the east, a series of walls and shallow ponds defining the west edge of the plaza and a glassy box gallery at the southwest corner. Reinforced concrete is used throughout the project to form continuously floating and folding surfaces to shape both the indoor galleries and outdoor display areas, and to frame the views of the surrounding city fragments.

Sculpted deeply into the ground, the building stretches horizontally to the outermost corners of the site. The flat surface of the site is remoulded, folded, fractured and warped to create a new urban geography. The whole plaza is divided into different geographic zones, such as hillside, stream, dry land and green slopes in response to the built geometry and the designated specific events. The design tries to blur the boundary of contrasting elements, such as building and plaza, indoor and outdoor, roof and ground, and so on.

This project provides an open public forum both for artists and the general public. The artificial landscape with maximum flexibility helps to define different zones for specific events. It also encourages artists to design site-specific sculptures and installations.

(All pictures supplied by project architects.)

3

4

3.4. Panoramic view

5. Ground floor plan

6. 1st floor plan

7. View from south of the plaza

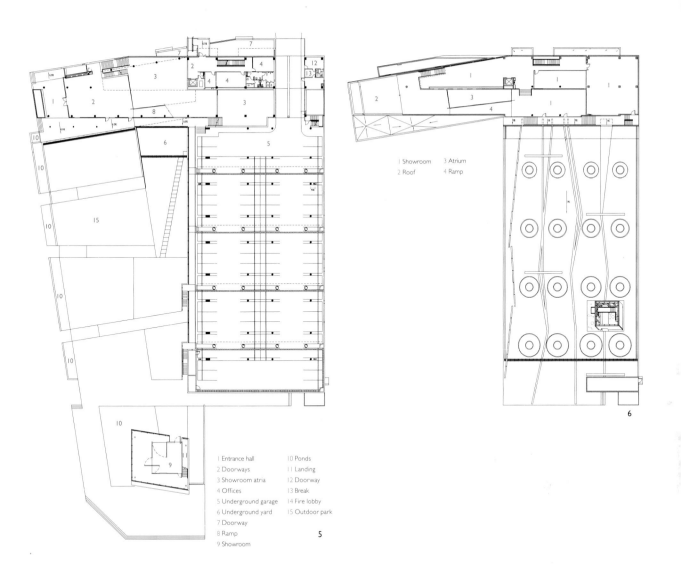

1 Showroom   3 Atrium
2 Roof   4 Ramp

1 Entrance hall   10 Ponds
2 Doorways   11 Landing
3 Showroom atria   12 Doorway
4 Offices   13 Break
5 Underground garage   14 Fire lobby
6 Underground yard   15 Outdoor park
7 Doorway
8 Ramp
9 Showroom

5

6

7

8. Lobby
9. Atrium from the ground floor
10. 1st floor gallery
11. Looking back to the lobby from the 1st floor gallery

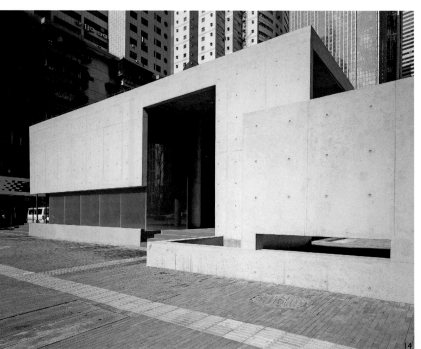

15

16

17

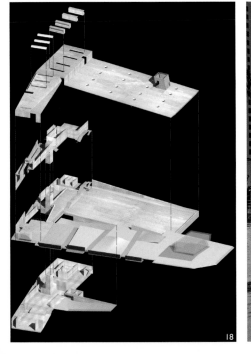

18

19

The Art and Design Building, Sichuan Academy of Fine Arts, Chongqing

Architect: Liu Jiakun

Location: Chongqing University Town, Shapingba

Floor area: 31,433 sqm

Design / Completion: 2005.10-2006.06 / 2006.06-2006.12

Architects: Liu Jiakun, Yang Ying, Chen Hong, Yang Lei,
Song Chunlai, Li Chun

Client: Sichuan Academy of Fine Arts

The Art and Design Building of Sichuan Academy of Fine Arts is situated on a hillside, surrounded by a mass of heavy industrial workshops, towering chimneys, obsolete buildings from the 1960s and 1970s, and contemporary buildings. The buildings are distributed in a triangular layout. It was decided that a group of single buildings could best adapt to the landforms. The buildings are provided, respectively, with arched ceilings, sloping roofs and V-shaped folded plate roofs. Looking up the slope, these buildings form a homogeneous and correlative form that seems to be guarding the hillside.

Liu Jiakun attempts to develop diverse buildings from the same architectural typology. The lecture buildings, broken up from a whole into parts, are scattered on several terraces with about 10 metres' height difference and in various positions. Despite the similar volumes and heights and the homogeneous materials, the buildings are endowed with rich and vivid expressions due to their unique roof compositions, collages of diverse materials, and external staircases. The functional differences do not always lead to differences in form. There is no simple correlation between the form and the function.

The seven buildings are generally square in form, except for the one with the double-sloped roof standing at the end and close to the driveway. One of its four sides is slightly inclined, which opens up the view. Wandering around, people may experience the diversification of angles and height differences between the buildings, as well as the various expressions of the façades. The two buildings facing the west are equipped with white vertical-slatted blinds in order to shelter them from the burning sunshine in the summer of Chongqing; while the others are clad in a combination of dark surfaces and glazing.

A series of diversifications have been made to the façades of the buildings. The two lecture buildings (A, B) parallel to the border of the site are equipped with vertical shades on the northwest façades facing the driveway. Five of the seven lecture buildings (A, B, D, E and G) are respectively inlaid with various collaged materials: perforated

1. Distant view of the seven buildings

bricks, galvanized sheets, corrugated cement sheets, ceramic veneers and cement shades; while the south and west façades of the other two buildings (C, F) are covered with red bricks and simply plastered. With regard to the windows, some are zonal windows, some are French windows, and some are simply discontinuous, large window openings. Some of the windows on different floors are aligned; some are not. Through collaging, apposing and intermixing, the architect constantly attempts to find as many schemes and combinations as possible in the construction.

The external staircases are different from each other. Some have overlapped projection planes, some are top-heavy, some are zig-zagging all over the gable wall and some are just segments.

(All pictures supplied by project architects. Photographer: Xu Lang, Deng Jing.)

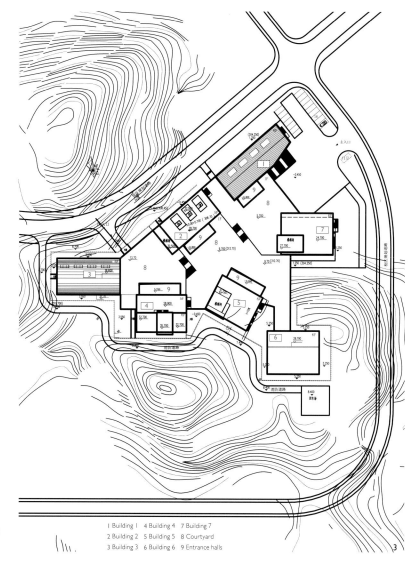

2. View of inner courtyard

3. Site plan

1 Building 1   4 Building 4   7 Building 7
2 Building 2   5 Building 5   8 Courtyard
3 Building 3   6 Building 6   9 Entrance halls

4

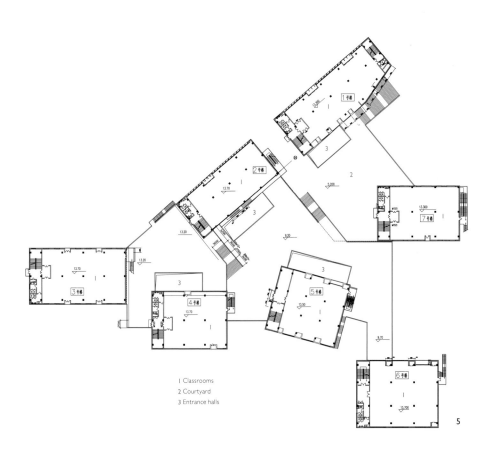

1 Classrooms
2 Courtyard
3 Entrance halls

5

4. 6. 7. 9. Views of inner courtyard

5. Plan at 13.3m

8. V-shaped folded-plate roof

6

7

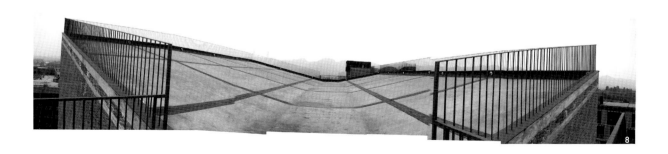

8

9

10.13. Exterior views
11.12.14. Exterior details

15. 16. 17. Exterior details

18. Courtyard

19. Platform and small yard
20. Interior space
21. 22. 23. 24. Hanging gable wall stairs

Sino-French Centre, Tongji University, Shanghai

Architects: Zhou Wei, Zhang Bin

Location: Main Campus of Tongji University, Shanghai
Design / Completion: 2004.03 / 2006.10
Area: 13,575 sqm
Architects: Zhou Wei, Zhang Bin, Zhuang Sheng, Lu Jun, Wang Jiaqi, Xie Jing
Client: Tongji University

1. Southeast view

The Sino-French Centre of Tongji University is located at the south-east corner of the campus, with the 12.9 Building, the oldest existing building on the campus, and 12.9 Memorial Park on its west side, the athletics field on its south side and Siping Road on its east side. The XuRi Building, which had to be preserved, is located at the north-west corner of the site. The other condition was that a group of existing metasequoias and the other scattered trees such as deodar cedars, planes, Japanese pagoda trees and willows were retained.

The goal of this project is to create a system to integrate its programme, its site context and its cultural context. The architects achieved this by using a geometric diagram to control the materialization of its programme and circulation, conformation to the site restrictions, and also to indicate its symbolic meaning – the cultural exchange between two countries.

The programme is composed of three parts: college, office and public gathering space. Two similar but different zig-zag volumes,

occupied by the college and the office sector respectively, overlap and interlace each other, and are linked together by the volume of the public gathering space on the underground and upper levels. The college and office sectors share the main entrance which is located at the void part of the intersection of these two volumes, while the public gathering space has its own lobby, which faces the roof pool and sunken garden, to connect the underground exhibition hall and the lecture hall on the upper level. The function of the college and offices is remembered through the use of regular shapes for almost every unit. But the application of zig-zag corridors to connect these units creates abundant interest throughout the inside and outside spaces. Existing trees are incorporated into the design to add even more charm to this complex.

Different materials and tectonics are applied to the different components of the complex. The college sector is clad in COR-TEN steel sheet panels. The unique texture and colour of the panels and

174

the smoothness of the glass create a delicate contrast. Pre-coated cement panels are introduced on the office sector. Regular and irregular bands of windows provide sunlight to the office units and corridors. Public gathering spaces are created by the combination of both COR-TEN steel panels and pre-coated cement panels. The vivid colour and texture of COR-TEN steel is contrasted with the plain grey cement panels. This treatment indicates the symbolic meaning of this project – the juxtaposition of two different cultures.

Landscape design plays a very important role in the project. The existing metasequoias, surrounded by the office sector, public gathering area and the XuRi Building, form an entry plaza to the complex. Connected with 12.9 Memorial Park, this will become a very important outdoor space to serve the entire campus. The connection between two parts of the building formed a roof pool and a sunken garden – an intermediary between urban space and campus space. A semi-private garden, created near the college and office sectors, provides a peaceful place for studying and relaxation.

Eventually, by applying different geometries, materials, colours and tectonics, a unique architectural piece was created that has a through and profound grasp of the meaning of cultural exchange between China and France.

(All pictures supplied by project architects. Photographer: Zhang Siye)

175

2. Overview

3. Main entrance lobby

4.5 Southeast view

1 Multi-functional hall
2 Office
3 Assembly room
4 Director´s office
5 Theatre
6 Teaching management office
7 Teachers´office
8 Classroom
9 Academic consultant´s room
10 Secretary
11 Copy and fax

12 Tea room
13 Storeroom
14 Toilets
15 Double-height space
16 Bridge
17 Atrium

17

1 XuRi Building
2 Entrance hall
3 Pond
4 140-seat classroom
5 Theatre
6 Classroom
7 Gatekeeper
8 Admissions
9 Training department
10 Toilets
11 Storeroom
12 Copy room
13 Tea room
14 Double-height space
15 Atrium

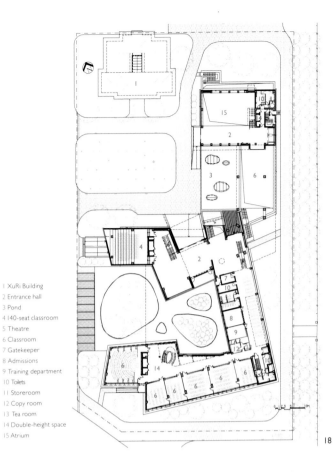

18

1 Showroom
2 Cafe
3 Preparation room
4 Atrium
5 Underground garage
6 Duty area
7 Toilets
8 Storeroom
9 Property stock room
10 Spares
11 Double-height space
12 Chief building distribution room
13 Transformer station
14 Ventilator room
15 Water control room
16 Pumping station
17 Water treatment

19

16. Sunken garden
17. 2nd floor plan
18. Ground floor plan
19. Basement plan

6. Staircase in college

7

7 Gallery on the 4th floor of the office section
8. Terrace on the 2nd floor of the public gathering area
9 Terrace on the ground floor of the college section

8

10.13. Public space of the college section

11. 12. 14. 15. Sections

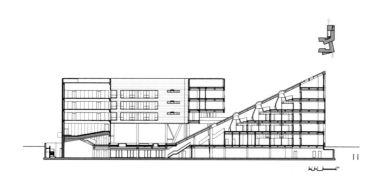

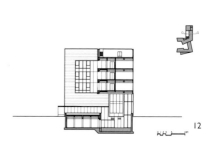

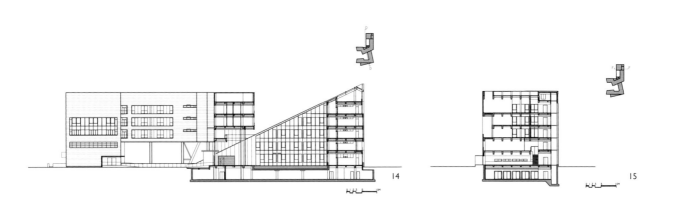

Suzhou Museum, Suzhou

Architect: I. M. Pei

Location: Suzhou
Design / Completion: 2002.06 / 2006.10
Area: 17,000 sqm
Architects: I. M. Pei Architects with Pei Partnership Architects (New York, NY /
Project), Suzhou Institute of Architectural Design Co. Ltd. Suzhou, China
Client: Suzhou Government

1. Main entrance

The new Suzhou Museum is located on an important historic and cultural block, neighbouring famous gardens such as the Humble Administrator's Garden and the Zhong Wang Fu, making it a challenge for the designer. On the basis of solid research and full comprehension of the local culture, I. M. Pei interprets the connotation of Suzhou traditional gardens with modern architectural language.

The new museum is in harmony with the original environment through its scattered layout. It is divided into three sections. As the main circulation space, the central part includes the entrance, the atrium, the central hall and the main garden; the west wing is the main exhibition area; the east wing includes the secondary exhibition area and the administration offices. The main garden adjoins the Humble Administrator's Garden to the north of the new museum. To the east, the Zhong Wang Fu (the former Suzhou Museum) has been rebuilt to become part of the new exhibition hall. Enjoying a harmonious co-existence, the new and the old buildings bring out the best in each

other. The design follows the principle that the volumes should be "not too high, not too large and not too abrupt". The project mainly consists of single-storey buildings and underground buildings. The cornice height of the main building is less than six metres; the two-storey buildings, positioned in the centre and the west, are far from the protected buildings, and do not exceed the height limit for the adjacent historic buildings. By such ingenious layout and rational scale control, the museum homogeneously blends into the original environment. In addition, streets near the museum have been repaired to revive their former appearance, which creates an atmosphere of traditional culture with an ancient flavour.

A lot of new technologies, new materials and new design techniques are applied in the design and construction of the new museum, which not only retains the traditional style of Suzhou gardens, but also exploits the features of modern architecture as a cutting-edge museum.

The steel structure, applied to the new museum, makes the

space and the layout free, open and bright. The traditional sloping roof is replaced by a geometric sloping roof, where the pyramidal glazing skylights in the solid geometrical frame are arranged at intervals. In addition, skylights are set up in the exhibition hall according to the various needs for natural lighting; wood-grain effect metal blinds are installed on the top of the hall and the corridor, as well as on the glazed roof and the high windows. Therefore, the natural light is diffused in the museum and varies with time. The museum is coloured black, white and grey, which are the main colours of traditional Suzhou buildings. Regarding the roof materials, "China Black" slates instead of tiles, cut into diamond shapes, are installed.

The main garden, the "soul" of the building, is placed in the centre, surrounded by museum buildings to the east, west and south, and adjoining the Humble Administrator's Garden to the north. The garden covers one fifth of the area of the museum. The garden has a water feature, which starts from the northwest corner of the north wall and seems to draw water from the Humble Administrator's Garden. A stone bridge crosses the water between the east and west banks. The most important feature in the garden is a group of rockeries which have the white wall of the Humble Administrator's Garden as a backdrop.

The Suzhou Museum is regarded by I. M. Pei as an experiment in developing Chinese architecture. On the one hand, a number of historic cities in China need to be preserved, while on the other hand, they also need to be developed. How to balance the preservation against the development is a task faced by Chinese architects. I. M. Pei hopes that his building will set an example, and encourage more architects to pay attention to the development of Chinese architecture.

(All pictures supplied by project architects.)

2. Panoramic view of the
courtyard

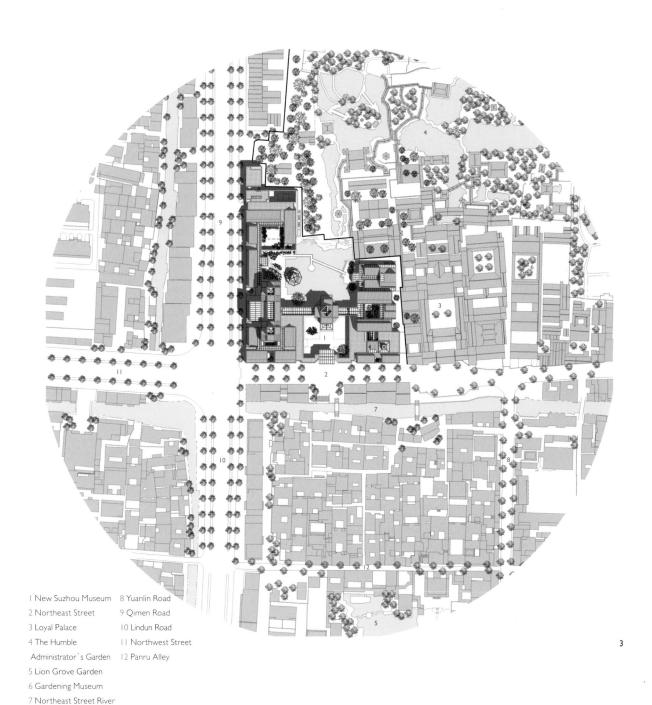

1 New Suzhou Museum   8 Yuanlin Road
2 Northeast Street   9 Qimen Road
3 Loyal Palace   10 Lindun Road
4 The Humble   11 Northwest Street
  Administrator's Garden   12 Panru Alley
5 Lion Grove Garden
6 Gardening Museum
7 Northeast Street River

3

3. Site plan
4. Entrance courtyard viewed through the
square window in the side corridor

5. Ground floor plan
6. Lobby

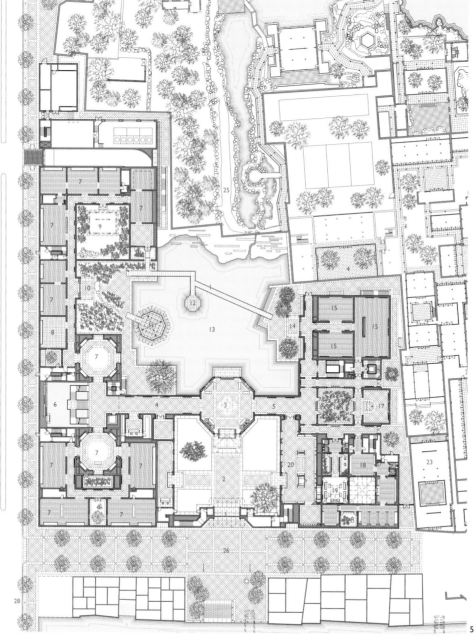

1 Main entrance
2 Main entrance hall
3 Hall
4 West corridor
5 East corridor
6 Lotus pond
7 Exhibition hall
8 Ming study room
9 Song picture room
10 West gate
11 Tea pavilion
12 Performance area
13 Main yard
14 East gate
15 Modern art exhibition hall
16 Ziteng cabinet
17 Cafe
18 Library
19 VIP reception area
20 Store
21 Ticket office
22 Cloakroom
23 Loyal Palace
24 Bibliotheca Building
25 The Humble Administrator's Garden
26 Northeast Street
27 Qimen Road
28 Lindun Road

5

7

7. Rock garden
8. Basement plan
9. 1st floor plan
10. Corridor beside the museum lobby

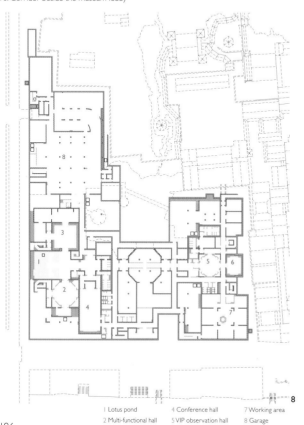

8

1 Lotus pond
2 Multi-functional hall
3 Exihibition hall
4 Conference hall
5 VIP observation hall
6 Assembly room
7 Working area
8 Garage

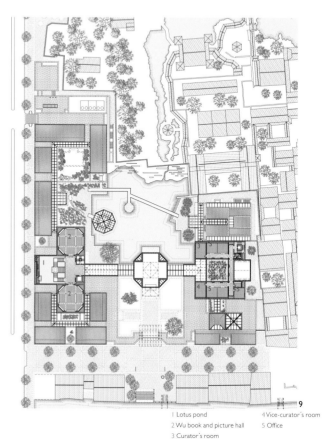

9

1 Lotus pond
2 Wu book and picture hall
3 Curator's room
4 Vice-curator's room
5 Office

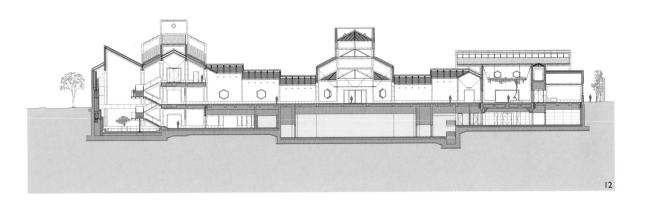

12

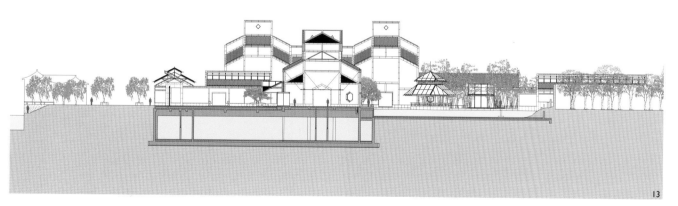

11. Courtyard viewed through bamboo

12.13. Sections

14. Exhibition hall for historical relics

15. Corridor

16. Rock garden viewed through the glass entrance

17. Exhibition hall for modern arts

18. Custom lighting fixture

19. Streetlamp

Wulongtan Resort, Ningbo

Architect: Bu Bing

Location: Wulongtan Scenic Area, Yinzhou District, Ningbo, Zhejiang Province
Design / Completion: 2003.10 / 2006.9
Area: 5,500 sqm
Architect: One Design
Client: YZCT, Ningbo

1. Overview of the resort

This resort hotel lies in a shallow valley about 400 metres long and 40 metres wide. A creek runs west to east through the whole site. A 5,500-square metre floor area is distributed across several buildings, including ten units of guest-room villas, one club house and some other functional buildings.

As the villas are sited in the middle of the valley, the roofs are designed to slope in different directions. Most living rooms overlook the creek, while the bedrooms are usually looking up at the sky. By breaking up these buildings, the narrow site appears to be enlarged.

The volume of the club house is unfolded by rotating the dining hall and the multi-function room above the creek. A camphor tree is preserved and rests comfortably in the centre of this newly formed courtyard. Glass curtain walls surrounding this courtyard bring the view of the valley and creek inside the building.

Compared to the vast volume of Siming Mountain, the building's area is trivial. This is why the buildings resist intentions of matching, balancing, or reacting against the natural landscape, but instead try to participate, as an observer, from the inside. Even if considered as part of the landscape, they are never the focal points. In the same way as the mountains, this group of buildings does not have to be seen all at once to be appreciated. The bildings seem to speak from the first person perspective, saying "we are inside this mountain".

Such a first-person perspective technique is frequently used in traditional Chinese landscape paintings or garden designs. The huts, fishers in the paintings, pavilions or bridges in the gardens are the subjects participating within the context rather than individual objects to be worshipped. In this way, multiple points of observation are formed; the huts and the pavilions entice the reader into the painting, or the visitor into the garden; they are looking around and at each other from within the landscape, at the same time but from multiple viewpoints. This kind of observation denies an exact depiction of the total in a single timeframe, but achieves more possibilities of reading with less limitation.

(All pictures supplied by project architects. Photographer: Cai Feng)

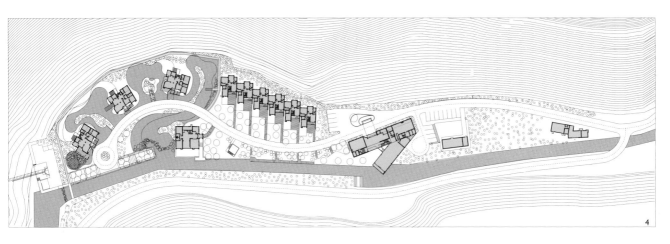

2. Pond between villa-type houses

3. Villa-type guest house

4. Site plan

5. Guest house in the valley

6. Row-house guest houses behind camphor trees

7. Elevation of guest house A

8. Sections of guest house A

9. Elevation of guest house B

10. West elevation of villa-type guest house B

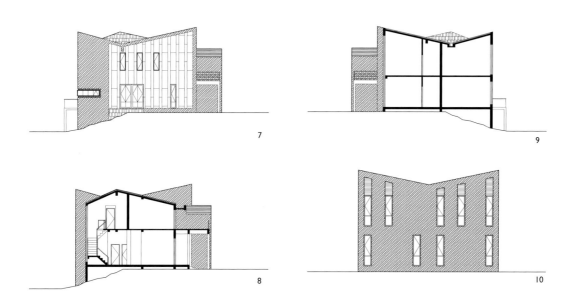

7

9

8

10

11. South elevation of row-house-type guest house C   14. South elevation of villa-type guest house B

12. West elevation of row-house-type guest house C

13. East elevation of row-house-type guest house C

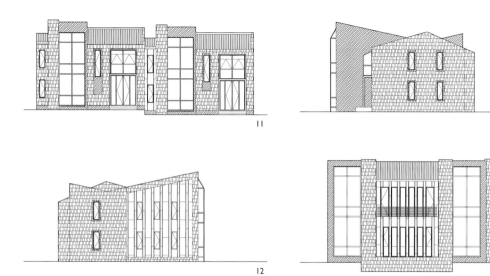

11

13

12

14

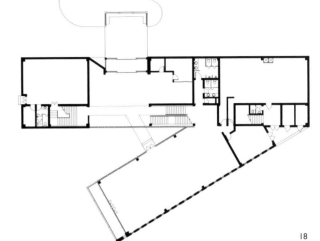

15. Courtyard in club house

16. Wooden bridge

17. Balcony above the creek

18. Ground floor plan

18

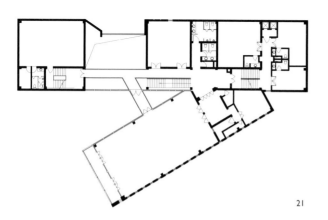

19. Creek-side facade

20. Row-house guest house

21. 1st floor plan

22. Pavilion on roof-top terrace

Hongluo Lake Club, Beijing

Architect: Ma Yansong

Location: Beijing

Area: 487 sqm

Design / Completion: 2006.06

Architects: Ma Yansong, Yosuke Hayano, Florian Pucher

Client: Beijing Dadi Real Estate Development Co., Ltd.

1. View from west

Hongluo Lake is an hour's drive away from downtown Beijing. Many villas sit around the lake in this beautiful area, and the famous Hongluo Temple is close by. A wooden bridge winds its way across the lake, and the Hongluo Club is situated on an irregular 487 square-metre platform in the middle of the bridge. The whole club seems to float on the lake, reflecting the surrounding mountains, and becoming a focal point for the area. Not only does the wooden bridge connect the club with the lake sides, it also provides another way of crossing the lake rather than the path around the edge. A continuous surface blurs the boundaries of the roof and the walls and, like the flowing water, it fluctuates and twists both horizontally and vertically. Several functions are separated, and then reconnected. Following the fluctuation of the surface you can enter two branched spaces in two directions: the sunken garden below the lake surface and a swimming pool floating in the lake. The sunken garden takes people to 1.3 metres below the lake surface. Walking across the garden makes you feel as if the lower half of your body is below the lake. Your eyes are at the same level as the lake's surface when you sit down. The swimming pool floating in the lake is also at the same level as the lake surface, and the boundary between them is blurred too.

The X-shaped spatial relationship is actually determined by the footprint of people as they move between functions of the building. Two major routes meet in the main body of the building, which is surrounded by a surface full of uncertainties that forms a rising three-dimensional organic structure and represents the instant transition from the liquid to the solid. During the course of the transition, the complex three-dimensional configuration becomes a thread connecting all the spaces.

All the vagueness and uncertainty of the spaces and functions are interesting topics. In an integrated space, different parts are endowed with distinct personalities, and there is no boundary between them. In those areas where the functions become vague, rules and order

break loose, receding from the industrial nature of modernism to get closer to natural rule. People are not forced to observe the order reflected by the space; they are actually encouraged to experience the space on their own and find a new order. The process might even involve the space-users' creativity and inspiration; their emotional and psychological input. This is an ever-changing architectural space, whose complex form does not only reflect the surroundings, but also becomes a junction where people and nature meet.

Unlike a modernist building, the Hongluo Lake Club is not concerned with how to connect urban architecture with nature, but rather about how architecture can give up the latent spatial order, and respond to the natural context with new logic to make the experience of the building one of being close to nature.

(All pictures supplied by project architects. Photographer: Shu He)

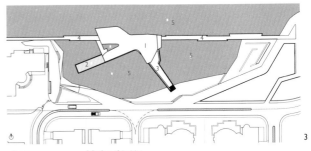

1 Club house
2 Outdoor swimming pool
3 Sunken square
4 Bridge
5 Surface of the lake

4

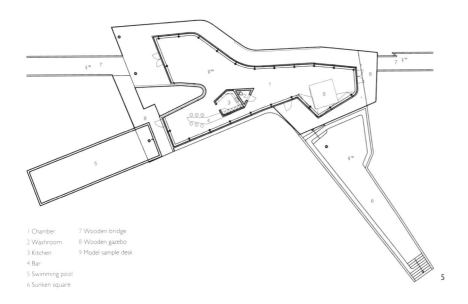

2.Club house with hidden passage

3.Site plan

4.Vista from open deck

5.Plan

1 Chamber	7 Wooden bridge
2 Washroom	8 Wooden gazebo
3 Kitchen	9 Model sample desk
4 Bar	
5 Swimming pool	
6 Sunken square	

5

6. South entrance under canopy

7. Section through beams

8. Sections

9. Interior space

10. 11. 12. Detail drawings

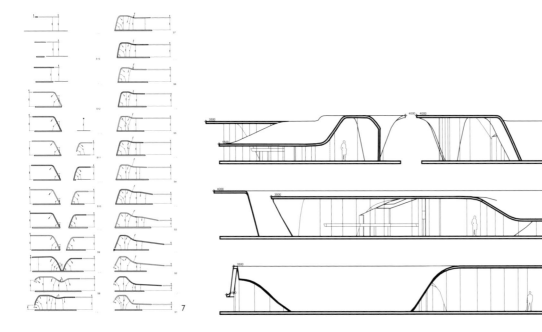

9

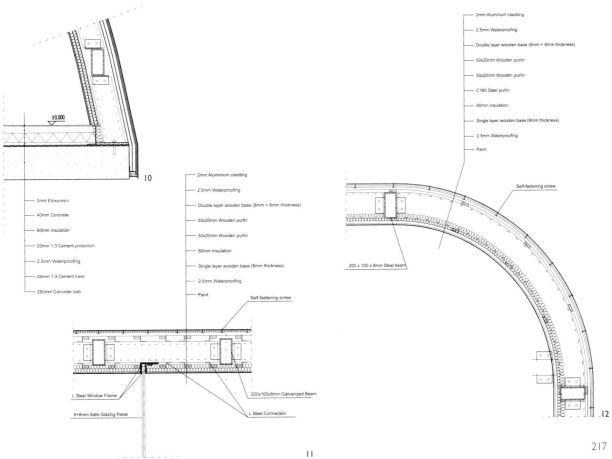

±0.000

10

- 2mm Etoxyresin
- 40mm Concrete
- 60mm Insulation
- 20mm 1:3 Cement protection
- 2.5mm Waterproofing
- 20mm 1:3 Cement base
- 250mm Concrete slab

- 2mm Aluminium cladding
- 2.5mm Waterproofing
- Double layer wooden base (8mm + 8mm thickness)
- 50x20mm Wooden purlin
- 50x20mm Wooden purlin
- 60mm Insulation
- Single layer wooden base (8mm thickness)
- 2.5mm Waterproofing
- Paint

Self-fastening screw

L Steel Window Frame

8+8mm Safe Glazing Panel

200x100x8mm Galvanized Beam

L Steel Connection

11

- 2mm Aluminium cladding
- 2.5mm Waterproofing
- Double layer wooden base (8mm + 8mm thickness)
- 50x20mm Wooden purlin
- 50x20mm Wooden purlin
- C160 Steel purlin
- 60mm Insulation
- Single layer wooden base (8mm thickness)
- 2.5mm Waterproofing
- Paint

Self-fastening screw

200 x 100 x 8mm Steel beam

12

Songzhuang Arts Centre, Beijing

Architect: Xu Tiantian

Location: Xiaopu Village, Songzhuang, Tongzhou District, Beijing
Design / Completion: 2005.04 / 2006.06
Area: 5,000 sqm
Architects: Xu Tiantian, Chen Yingnan, Zhu Junjie (DnA Studio)
Client: Council of Xiaopu Village, Songzhuang, Beijing

Songzhuang Arts Centre is located in Xiaobu village, Songzhuang town, in a Beijing suburb, which is invested in by the council of the village and covers an area of 5,000 square metres. It was the first work completed by DnA (Design and Architecture) Studio following its launch two years previously. The centre is situated on unused industrial land in the northwest corner of Xiaobu village. Similar to other emerging towns in China, the village seems to be lacking in an effective city context. Besides the scattered industrial workshops, there is only the broad and flat land, but that did not prevent the architect from acquiring inspiration from this ordinary village. The design of the centre, from exterior form to interior meaning, and even the materials, is abstracted from the image of Xiaobu village. Through simple architectural language and with special consideration of the environment, space, structure and material aspects, the architect puts emphasis on the harmonious co-existence between the environment and the architecture, and promotes the merging of contemporary aesthetics and local culture.

The first, attractive image of the centre is the walls made of red sliced clay bricks, providing a surface that is integrated, bright and lively. From afar, the building appears as a huge red rock that rises above the ground, while on closer inspection, it appears as a huge red box floating on the square. On the ground floor there are glass enclosures that are thin and highly transparent, so the original sense of heaviness and gravity is replaced by a sense of flotation. When passing the glass wall at the entrance, the material changes from red brick to the white walls of the indoor space. The indoor exhibition spaces, including the courtyard and the exhibition hall on the first floor, are white. The white self-levelling floor, together with the white wall, retains the purity of the art exhibition space. On the ground floor, the small accessory space is covered with OSB, which implies an industrial feature. Its bright yellow texture gives the visitors a little bit of visual surprise. DnA has made transitions between the volume and

218

1. Exterior view
2. Site plan

the heaviness of the unadorned material, which not only highlights the visual effect of the architecture, but also evokes the dense rural buildings in and around Songzhuang.

According to the design concept of the Songzhuang Arts Centre, the building is characterized by the sense of volume, specific space division and clearly discernible functions. Spaces are arranged vertically instead of horizontally. On the ground floor is a diaphanous and horizontally flowing space, which can either be a small, flowing exhibition space or a comfortable interaction space such as a café or bookshop. Accessory spaces such as offices, storerooms, plant rooms and toilets are respectively compressed in small, scattered boxes. Three main exhibition halls and the academic hall are situated on the first floor and are definitely enclosed. The enclosures are exhibition walls, but also act as insulation. The ground and first floors are connected by a vertical space, encouraging the overlapping of and transition between the two levels. The vertical space, either a high

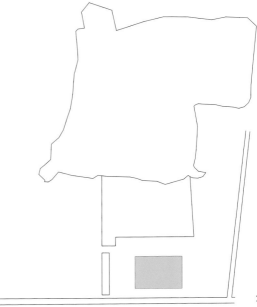

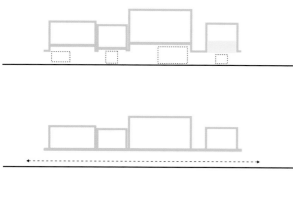

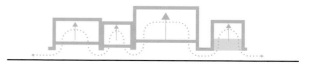

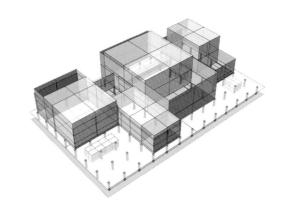

4

3

3. Concept of volumes
4. Concept of circulation
5. Analytical 3D model
6. Projecting eaves of the entrance

5

hall that connects the two levels or a courtyard that enjoys natural lighting and ventilation, provides visual communication between the inside and the outside. The design of the centre, including its vertical connections and lengthways slits, provides exhibition planning with more alternatives. Its large-scale space meets the requirements of various exhibition formats.

Placing more emphasis on the sense of volume than the sense of format, the architect of the centre tried to avoid creating overly formal architecture; however, this does not mean rough design and neglect of detail treatment. Take the design of the steel stairs as an example: many 2mm × 2mm square pipes of different lengths are woven between the 0.3-metre wide girders. Just as if creating an artwork, each square pipe was positioned by the architect personally on site.

(All pictures supplied by project architects.)

7. Staircase in exhibition hall

8. Exterior view

9. Sections

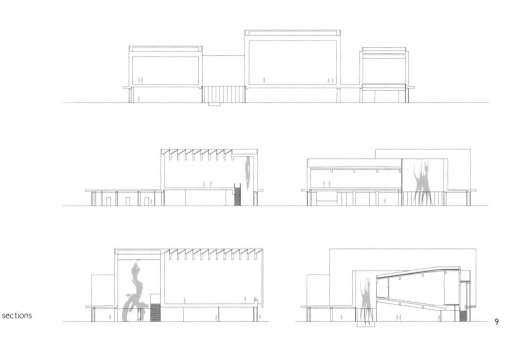

sections

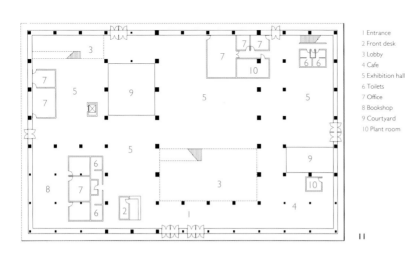

1 Entrance
2 Front desk
3 Lobby
4 Cafe
5 Exhibition hall
6 Toilets
7 Office
8 Bookshop
9 Courtyard
10 Plant room

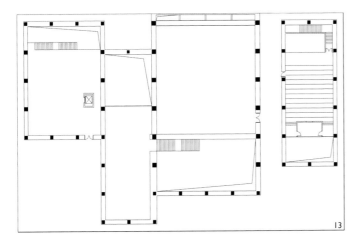

10. View of exhibition hall

11. Ground floor plan

12. View of exhibition hall

13. 1st floor plan

14. Partial view of courtyard

15. Roof terrace

"GEMHEART Yuan Jie", Chengdu

Architect: Liu Jiakun

Location: Chengdu, Sichuan province

Design / Completion: 2004.09-2005.05 / 2005.06-2006.05

Area: 29,462.9 sqm

Architects: Liu Jiakun, Wang Lun, Yang Ying, Song Chunlai

Client: Sichuan Dingxin Real Estate Co., Ltd.

    Chengdu Long Wei Industrial Co., Ltd.

"GEMHEART Yuan Jie" is located in a sensitive area of Chengdu, close to the famous Kuangxiangzi Alley and Zhaixiangzi Alley, two conservation districts of historic sites; and also next to recently completed high-rise commercial complexes.

GEMHEART Yuan Jie is situated between the old district and the new district along a curved path. Liu Jiakun's composition, with "surface" as the basic unit carried by a U-shaped courtyard, responds to the relationship between the two sides of a "space-time transition" with the relationship of a mirror image reversal between convex and concave. The void spaces, as if stitched by a zip, are turned into an entity, while the void spaces become available as visual channels or traffic passages. The façade of GEMHEART Yuan Jie facing the old district is discontinuous and irregular. The other side, facing the high-rise commercial complex, has a mass of continuous interfaces inserted, and the irregularity increases above ground level.

As to the vertical dimension and the traffic system construction,

Liu Jiakun achieves his goal by various architectural techniques: making the four-storey high GEMHEART Yuan Jie the transition from the traditional block buildings to the high-rise housing and office buildings; extending the main streets of traditional blocks to form crossing paths and bridge galleries; and constructing a U-shaped hanging street on the second level of the buildings.

Liu Jiakun treats the sloping roof as follows: 1) Keeping the ridge line horizontal, different from the folding and topological deformation used by some Western architects, "to keep the ridge of a traditional sloping roof is the premise of deformation"; 2) Simplifying the traditional relationship between the sloping roof and wall by omitting the eaves, making a direct transition between roof and walls; 3) Changing the parallel relationship between the ridge line and the eaves by using oblique lines and broken lines that show a sharp contrast with the ridge line; 4) Replacing the traditional roofing material – terrace tiles – with modern concrete slabs.

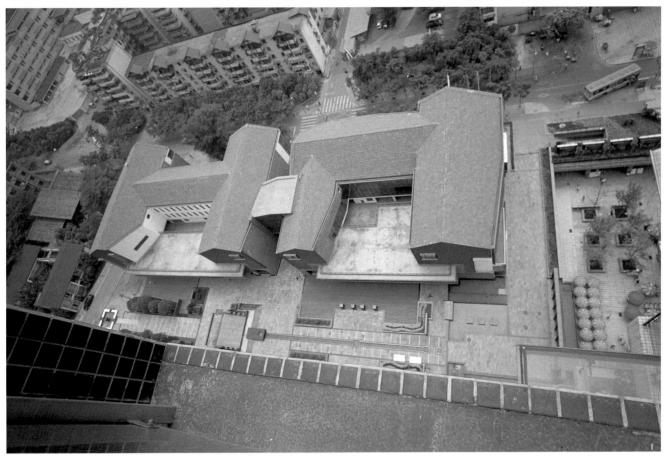

1. Overview

As for the treatment of the walls, Liu Jiakun adopts the use of materials researched on the ceramic hall and fresco hall in the second phase of Mrgadava Museum; replacing blue brick with pre-cast concrete. The pre-cast concrete blocks, custom-made in a local cement building materials factory, are laid parallel, and clearly form a horizontal recessed gap. The horizontal recessed gap and the hidden perpendicular gap perform the function of waterproofing, which is the result of integration of processing technology, material function, cost control and prefabrication. It also contrasts with the craft and visual effect of traditional brick masonry.

Moreover, the design of the "skin", with more directness and stronger visual effect, is about the aluminium alloy grid. The form of the grid seems to be the opposite of the relationship between the gaps and bricks in a the traditional plain brick wall, which produces a penetration effect like a hollow window lattice. The red organic glass lamps interspersed on the grid dissolve the integrated framework. In the daytime they implicitly indicate the commercial nature of the building, while in the evening they present the atmosphere of nightlife.

(All pictures supplied by project architects.)

2. Exterior view

3. Inside view of the bridge gallery

4.5. Model

6. Site plan

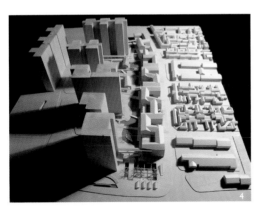

7. Details of the façade
8. Ground floor plan
9. 1st floor plan
10. 2nd floor plan
11. Exterior view of the bridge gallery

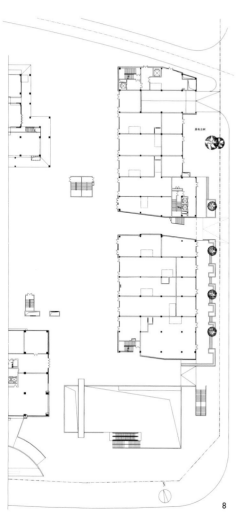

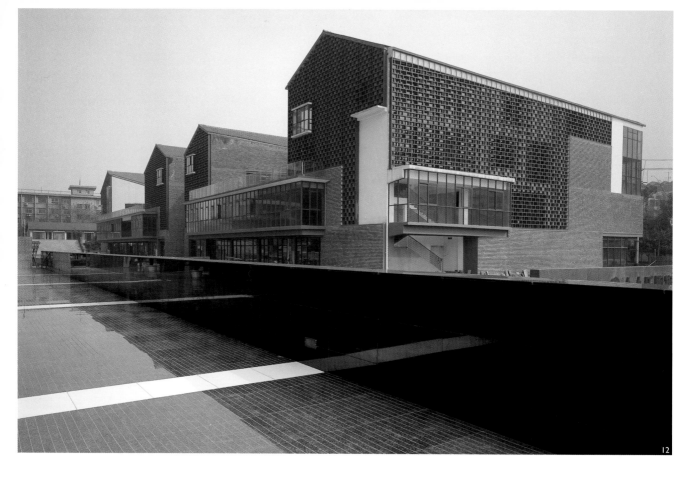

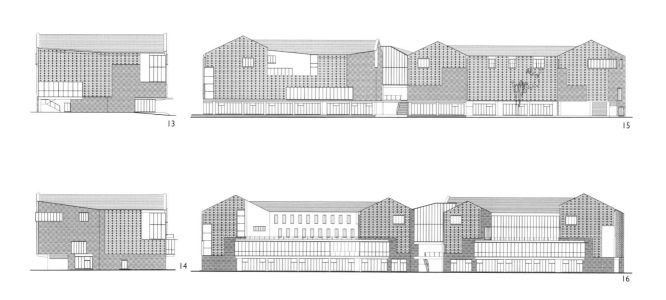

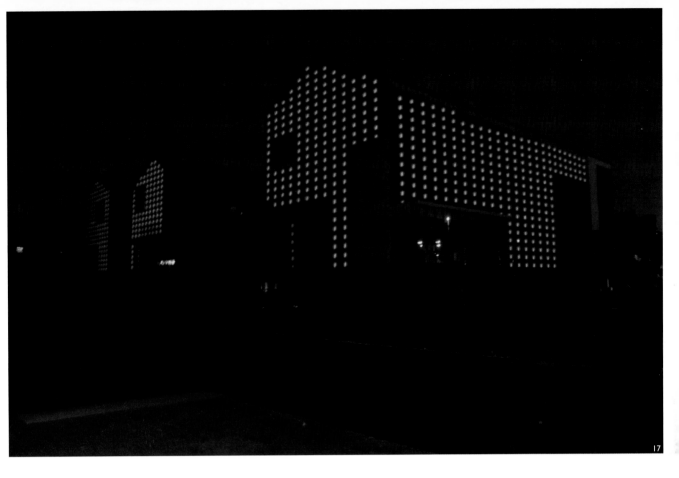

12.17. Overall view in daylight and at night
13. 14. 15. 16. Elevations
18.19. Sections

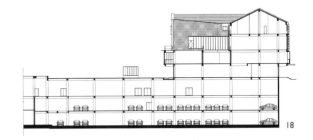

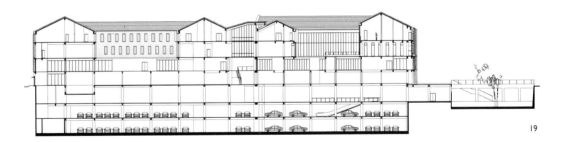

China National Offshore Oil Corporation Headquarters, Beijing

Architect: Kohn Pedersen Fox Associates (KPF)

Location: Chaoyang Men, Dongcheng District, Beijing
Design / Completion: 2006.04
Area: 96,340 sqm
Architect: Kohn Pedersen Fox Associates (KPF)
Client: China National Offshore Oil Corporation

1. General view from southeast

The China National Offshore Oil Corporation Headquarters is located at the northwest of the Chaoyangmen Overpass, Dongcheng district, Beijing, facing the massive Ministry of Foreign Affairs building at the southeast corner across the overpass. In a light but aggressive shape, the triangular building inclines towards the street corner. The angle of the building shades the north side from sunlight, enriches the streetscape visually, and creates more interesting squares and communal spaces for the building and the city.

Designed by KPF, the building is in an equilateral triangle in plan, with rounded corners, and the tapering of the tower is narrower at the bottom and wider at the top. The dynamic landscaped square at the south of the tower make the entrance more interesting. Thanks to the geometrical purity of this symbolic shape, the tower stands out from the surrounding noisy environment, and becomes a landmark within the limit height of 80 metres, as well as a vivid reflection of the concept of "less is more".

Designed by KPF, the glazed ceramic panel system from Germany is installed on the exterior walls of the building and the sides of the tower, which naturally recalls the traditional clay used in Beijing. The materials and colours of those illustrious buildings are recalled by the meticulous application of modern materials. Another symbolic part of the tower is the 70-metre wide grand "flying eaves" at the entrance to the Western courtyard, which symbolizes the gateway of the Chinese traditional gardens.

Within the tower, the architects provide the staff members with flowing and comfortable rest and communication spaces by setting up a triangular, sunlit atrium at the centre. On the three sides of the tower, according to the sun path, KPF has arranged three vertical sky gardens that differ in form, area and location. Sunlight penetrates the atrium horizontally through the gaps between the gardens. Such a delicate arrangement not only provides the small teams of the corporation with scattered meeting spaces, but also gives the occupants of the building a sense of orientation and passing time.

In order to interpret the spatial relations between the three

2. View of the west façade and the grand gate

3. 13.7-metre high glass lobby enclosure with stainless steel tension truss supports

4. Entry lobby

5. Entry diagram

6. Conceptual sketch showing the sun path around the building in plan

gardens and the whole building, KPF defines their outlines using transparent and translucent glazing on the façade and the gaps between the ceramic blinds in the atrium.

(All pictures supplied by project architects. Fig 1–4, 12 Photographer: H.G.Esch; Fig 10, 13 Photographer: Zhang Guangyuan.)

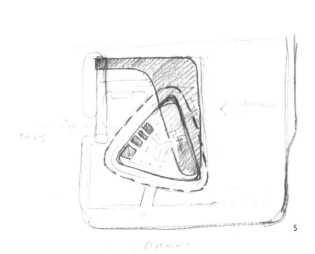

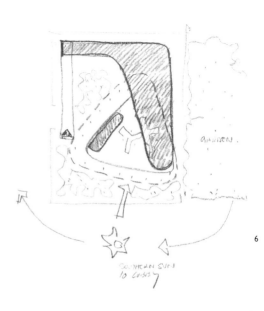

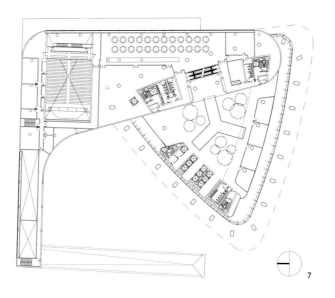

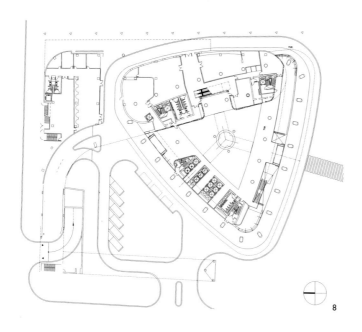

7. Ground floor plan

8. 2nd floor plan

9. 10th floor plan

10. Atrium skylight seen from below

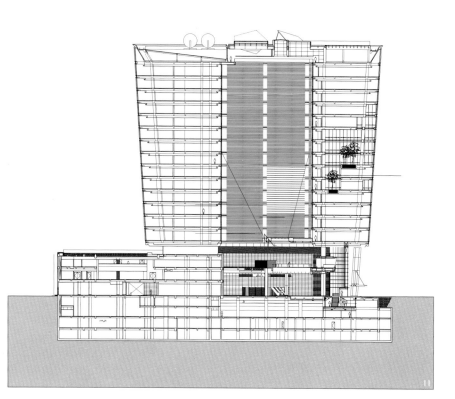

Jinhua Architecture Park, Zhejiang

Architect: Ai Weiwei

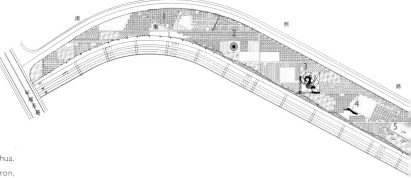

Location: Jindong New District of Jinhua, Zhejiang Province
Design / Completion: 2004.09 / 2006.02
Area: 3,000 sqm
Planners: Jindong New District Construction Department of Jinhua,
Zhejiang Province; Beijing FAKE Design; Herzog & de Meuron,
Switzerland
Architects: Till Schweizer (Germany), Christ / Gantenbein (Germany),
Tatiana Bilbao (Mexico), Herlach / Hartmann / Frommenwiler
(Switzerland), Liu Jiakun. Wang Xingwei / Xu Tiantian, Buchner
Bründler Architekten BSAAG (Switzerland), Ding Yi / Chen
Shuyu, Wang Shu, Ai Weiwei, Toshiko Mori (Japan), Erhard An-He
Kinzelbach (Germany), Fün Design Consultancy (Holland), Fernando
Romero (Mexico), Herzog & de Meuron (Switzerland), Michael
Maltzan (U.S.A.), Yungho Chang
Client: Jindong New District Department of Jinhua, Zhejiang Province

The Jinhua Architecture Park is an important part of the greenbelt in Jindong New Developing District, Jinhua, Zhejiang Province, which covers an area of 14.9 hectares, with a length of 2,200 metres and an average width of 80 metres. In the park, there are 17 urban public mini-structures designed by 17 architectural groups and artists from seven countries, such as Ai Weiwei and Herzog & de Meuron. Each of the structures covers an area that ranged from a few dozen square metres to 300 square metres, totalling 3,000 square metres. The park landscape is designed by Ai Weiwei.

Green spaces are set up along the side roads in order to break away from the narrow zone. Instead of being scattered, familiar vegetation is planted in nursery gardens and avenues, different from the arrangement in traditional parks.

No. 1: Welcome Centre designed by Till Schweizer, Germany. Its core, which has no direct relation to the exterior façade, guides people to the roof terrace to enjoy the view. The exterior façade is a wooden reticulation, which specifies the form of the architecture in appearance.

No. 2: Tea House designed by Christ/Gantenbein, Architekten ETH/SIA, Germany. It looks like a tree, and provides space for people to relax and enjoy leisure time.

No. 3: Exhibition Space designed by Tatiana Bilbao, Mexico. With free and vivid form, it is composed of random helixes and fold lines. Its spaces, sections and parts keep changing and twisting.

No. 4: Kids' Playground designed by HHF, Switzerland. It is a pavilion with reinforced concrete structure, which allows children different ways of playing by means of flexible, multi-layered structures such as various combinations of complex openings on the walls.

No. 5: Tea House designed by Liu Jiakun, China. The architect designed the structure in a simple and easy way, which makes its form highly explicit.

No. 6: Toilets designed by Wang Xingwei and Xu Tiantian, China. Male or female, interior or exterior, the structure is characterized by

1 Welcome Centre
2 Ancient Tree
3 Exhibition room
4 Baby Dragon
5 Tea House
6 Toilets
7 Management room
8 Internet Cafe
9 Café-China House
10 Archaeological archive
11 News Stand
12 Multi-media Space
13 Restaurant
14 Bridging Tea House
15 Virtual library
16 Book Bar
17 Pavilion

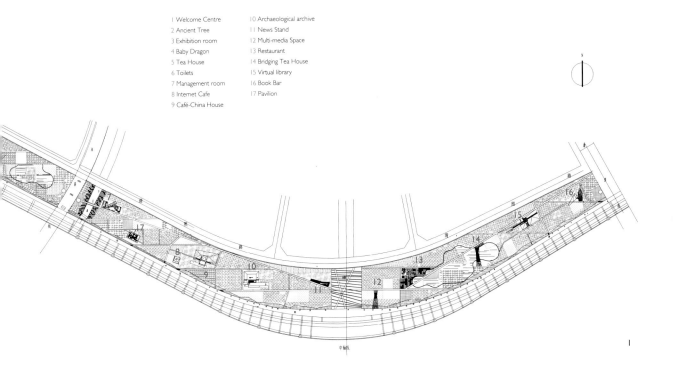

these basic concepts about the toilet.

No. 7: The Manager Room designed by Buchner Bründler Architekten BSAAG, Switzerland. The layout is similar to the retaining wall that is popular in China. Diversified buildings and bounding walls are artfully put together to enclose three courtyards.

No. 8: Internet Café designed by Ding Yi and Chen Shuyu, China. In shape, it is a basic square body. With specified paths and enclosing walls, this 12m x 12m space is provided with pathways, screen walls and courtyards, which cover all the features of a traditional Chinese garden.

No. 9: Coffee House designed by Wang Shu, China. A relationship has been built between the form of the park and the structures by rebuilding the surrounding environment. Meanwhile, the simplification in shape contrasts with the extreme treatment of the surface.

No. 10: Pottery Art Museum designed by Ai Weiwei, China. The building takes its form from the double-sloping roofed house that is popular locally. Three houses with sloped roofs are put together, which

forms a hexagonal section. Looking at the museum from the east, west and south, it appears to be a normal building with a sloping roof. Only when looking at it from the north do its unique features unfold.

No. 11: Newspaper Stand designed by Toshiko Mori, Japan. Its exterior space becomes part of the building. Its spatial form is interpreted by a single wall, pathways around the wall, spaces at both sides of the wall and the newspaper display.

No. 12: Multi-media Space designed by Erhard An-He Kinzelbach, Germany. It is a profiled space made by cast in-situ reinforced concrete. It shows great integrity, for its exterior form, interior space and structure are completed in the same architectural language.

No. 13: Restaurant designed by Fün Design Consultancy, Netherlands. Its form is similar to the overhead building structure, one of the Chinese traditional structures. Just like the pavement snack booth popular in Zhejiang and Jiangsu province, it is easily accessible from all directions.

1. 2. 3. Welcome Centre

No. 14: Bridge Tea House designed by Fernando Romero, Mexico. The building, with a bridging structure across the water, creates a relatively hyper-realistic state in the context of the park.

No. 15: Reading Space designed by Herzog & de Meuron, Switzerland. It is a complicated spatial structure, which is vertically extended from its basic plane form that looks like a piece of Chinese folk paper-cut for window decoration.

No. 16: Book Bar designed by Michael Maltzan, United States. The architect creates a special way of feeling about interior and exterior spaces through the shape of the design.

No. 17: Pavilion designed by Yungho Chang, China. The design concept attempts to strengthen the original concept in microcosm for the structures in the park: a group of 17 structures similar to the original ones that are one tenth of the original size.

(All pictures supplied by project architects.)

4. 5. Tea House

6

6. 7. 8. Baby Dragon

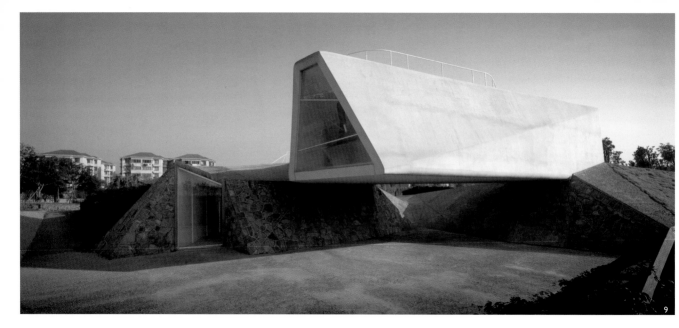

9

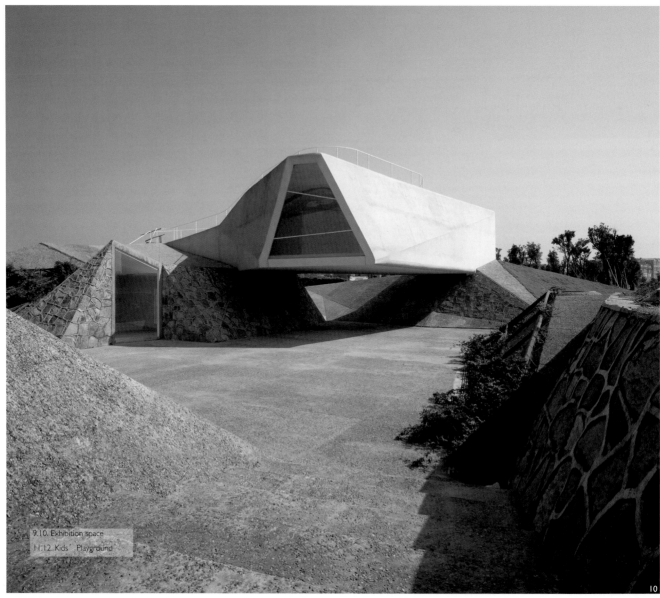

9.10. Exhibition space
11.12. Kids' Playground

10

13. 14. 15. Tea House

16. 17. Toilets

18. 19. Management room
20. 21. Internet Cafe

20

21

22. 23. Newspaper Stand
24. 25. Book Bar

25

26

27

28

26. 27. 28. 29. Pottery Art Museum
Archive

29

30. 31. Multi-media Space
32. 33. Restaurant

34

35

34. 35. Bridging Tea House
36. 37. Reading space

265

38. 39. 40. 41. Book Bar

39

40

41

42

42. 43. 44. Pavilion

43

Z58, Shanghai

Architect: Kengo Kuma

Location: 58 Panyu Road, Shanghai
Design / Completion: 2003 / 2006
Area: 4,000 sqm
Architects: Kengo Kuma & Associates, China Fanhua Group
Client: Zhongtai Holding Group

1. East elevation

Z58 is located on Panyu Road in Shanghai, with four storeys above ground. It faces the Panyu Road with its glazed exterior wall set with planters of highly polished stainless steel at regular intervals. The façade captures images mirrored on the shiny stainless steel planters and the view from the inside, seen through lianas and glazing, integrates the inside and outside. Rather than confronting the street with a wall, the relationship between architecture and city represented here is that the architecture blends into the street as though by osmosis.

The entrance is inconspicuous at the corner of the façade. Passing the entrance hall, visitors will reach a glazed atrium open to the highest level. When arriving at this space, they will then understand that the glazed façade with planters is not the real exterior wall of the building, but a wall set up separately from the building within for the purpose of facing the city. The real exterior wall facing the atrium is also glazed. On its surface, glazing bars are arranged at regular intervals, and water streams down the whole façade from the top, like a waterfall curtain. Under the wall is a pool, which makes visitors feel as if they are approaching an island.

The lift (also with a glazed skin) at the heart of the atrium connects each floor. On the ground floor there are shops and negotiation spaces; on the first floor there is an exhibition area; on the second floor there are offices; and on the third floor there are guest rooms and recreational spaces.

Loosely arranged in the office area on the second floor, offices and meeting rooms are separated from each other without blocking the view by glazed partitions or walls. At the fourth floor, guest rooms, lounge and café are placed on the water. Sitting in an Eames lounge chair in the water lounge between guest rooms and café, visitors are given a view of the Hispanic-style houses to the south, and also overlook the urban landscape of Shanghai.

The current layout of the third floor was arrived at for a

2

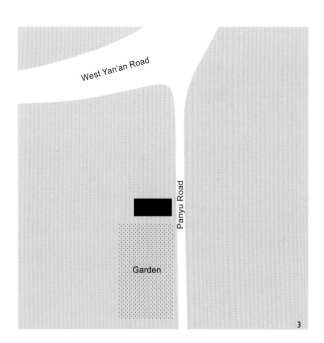

West Yan'an Road

Panyu Road

Garden

3

particular reason. As a matter of fact, Z58 is not a newly completed building. It was formerly a clock factory, a three-storey building of reinforced concrete structure. The Japanese architect Kengo Kuma has retained almost all the reinforced concrete structure, and then added the third floor on the top. Therefore, now the ground to the second floors are of the former reinforced concrete structure, while the third floor and the atrium – the steel structures – have been added, along with the element of water.

(All pictures supplied by client. Fig. 1, 2, 4, 5, 13, 16 photographer: Fujitsuka Mitsumasa; Fig. 12, 19 photographer: Wang Dagang.)

4

2. Exterior view

3. Site plans

4. Night view of south facade

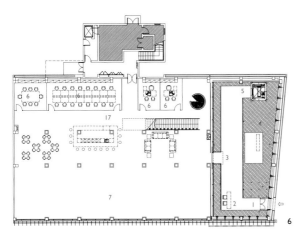

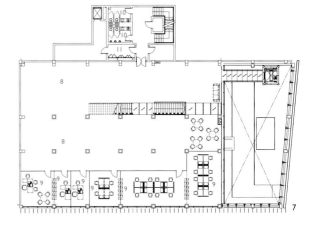

1 Entrance	6 Meeting room	11 Distribution room	16 VIP meeting room	21 Bar
2 Reception	7 Exhibition room	12 Reading room	17 Toilets	22 Multi-functional hall
3 Lobby	8 Showroom	13 Assembly room	18 Changing room	23 Reading room
4 Pond	9 Office	14 Open-plan office	19 Wine cellar	24 Gymnasium
5 Lift	10 Toilets	15 Office	20 Kitchen	25 Sauna room

26 Guest room	
27 Water bar	
28 Pilotis	
29 Toilets	

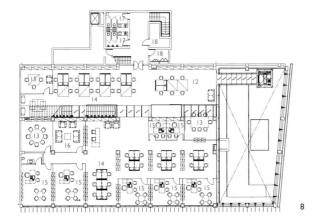

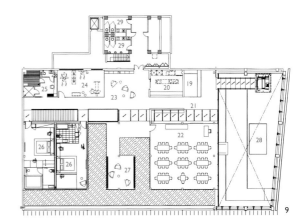

5. Atrium

6. Ground floor plan

7. 1st floor plan

8. 2nd floor plan

9. 3rd floor plan

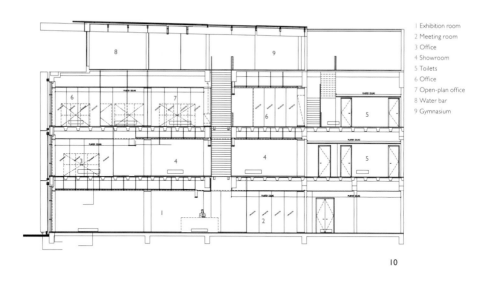

1 Exhibition room
2 Meeting room
3 Office
4 Showroom
5 Toilets
6 Office
7 Open-plan office
8 Water bar
9 Gymnasium

10

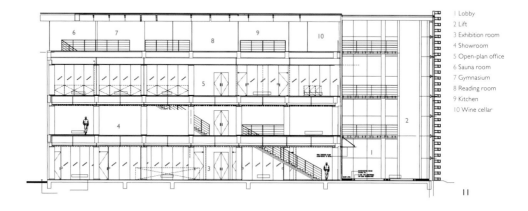

1 Lobby
2 Lift
3 Exhibition room
4 Showroom
5 Open-plan office
6 Sauna room
7 Gymnasium
8 Reading room
9 Kitchen
10 Wine cellar

11

10. 11. Sections
12. Atrium

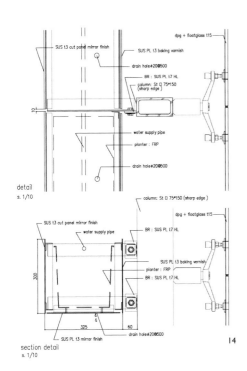

SUS t3 cut panel mirror finish
SUS PL t3 baking varnish
drain hole φ20@500
BR : SUS PL t7 HL
column: St □ 75*150 (sharp edge)
water supply pipe
planter : FRP
drain hole φ20@500
dpg + floatglass t15

detail
s. 1/10

SUS t3 cut panel mirror finish
water supply pipe
column: St □ 75*150 (sharp edge)
BR : SUS PL t7 HL
dpg + floatglass t15
SUS PL t3 baking varnish
planter : FRP
BR : SUS PL t7 HL
300
325   60
SUS PL t3 mirror finish
drain hole φ20@500

section detail
s. 1/10

14

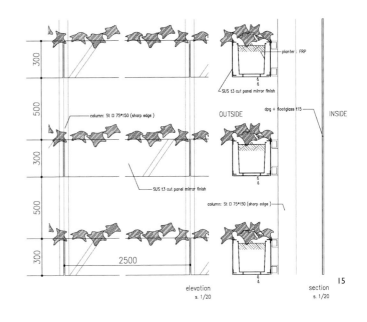

300
500
300
500
300

column: St □ 75*150 (sharp edge)

SUS t3 cut panel mirror finish

2500

planter : FRP
SUS t3 cut panel mirror finish
dpg + floatglass t15
column: St □ 75*150 (sharp edge)

OUTSIDE   INSIDE

elevation
s. 1/20

section
s. 1/20

15

13. Detail of skin
14. Detail of planters
15. Elevation and section of planters
16. Water pavilion on top floor

16

17. 18. 19. Offices

Museum of Art, Ningbo

Architect: Wang Shu

Location: Ningbo, Zhejiang province

Completion: 2006

Area: 23,100 sqm

Architect: Wang Shu

The Ningbo Museum of Art is converted and rebuilt from a port control building, which used to be the landmark building of the city during the 1970s and 1980s. Many citizens came here to board ships leaving for Shanghai or for Putuo to burn joss-sticks. As a typical downtown port, it was situated beside a cluster of colonial-style buildings. This area in Ningbo is comparable to Shanghai's famous Bund district.

It was originally planned that the port control building would be renovated; its large waiting space was perfect for large-scale exhibition of contemporary artworks. However, having been redecorated and repaired several times, its prefabricated concrete structure could no longer meet the standard of earthquake-proof design. In order to be consistent with the architectural style of the city, the architect proposed to rebuild the building as if protecting an old building, and keep the interior spatial structure the same, because the image of the interior space has been impressed on the memories of Ningbo people for generations. The final scheme integrates the considerations on various sites. The high entrance platform along the urban arterial road and the steel-timber structure beside the river, being shaped like rectangles, parallel to each other and lying beside the river, are reminiscent of of ships and docks along the Yong River. On the side that faces the city, they imply and represent the Chinese traditional urban courtyards and urban structures. When entering the museum, people must first pass through a raised courtyard with a zig-zag entrance ramp. There is no normal public square or great step at the side of the building that faces the street, which has caused many disputes during the process of design and construction. In fact, the designer's purpose is to represent the ceremonial style of Chinese urban life. In the early morning, people walk up the courtyard, pass through a landing stage across the building, and then enter the riverside corridor on the first floor. In this 100-metre long, 8-metre high and 6-metre wide space, 100 eight-metre high doors

1. West view of the museum
from the raised courtyard

made of fir open gradually at the same time. Sunlight and the view of the Yong River fill the space, lending a sense of ceremony.

Another typical feature of the museum is the two-stage process in the vertical direction, which reflects the needs of functions and economy in Chinese traditional and contemporary cities. The lower stage indicates the "economic base". Under the raised courtyard at the entrance, a large garage that can park 150 cars is positioned in order to meet the explosive future car-parking needs in the city. Inside the blue-brick base under the main building, a 2,000 square metre open exhibition hall is placed, which can be used for exhibition activities such as art fairs. By this means, the common problem faced by museums in Chinese cities – lack of money for operations and maintenance beyond the construction input – can be solved. The upper levels are "superstructure", and are used for various exhibitions of fine arts.

The materials used for the skin of the building also imply the mix of memories in the city. The blue brick used for the base is traditionally the main building material in Ningbo, while the steel and timber are materials mainly used for building ships and ports. The design of grottoes on the blue-brick base beside the river is copied from Dunhuang Caves, which implies that here, still, is the departure place for Ningbo people to go to Putuo to burn joss-sticks.

(All pictures supplied by project architects. Fig 1, 2, 4-6, 11-13, 17, 23 © Lü Hengzhong; Fig 9, 10 © Peng Nu.)

2

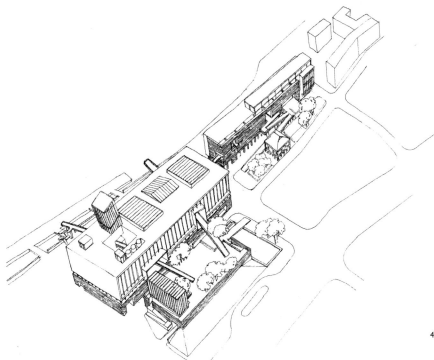

2. East view of the museum

3. Main lobby

4. Sketch by architect Wang Shu

9. View of the main facade of museum from the raised courtyard

6. Overview of the museum

7. Mezzanine plan of the 1st floor

8. 1st floor plan

9. 10. Walkway between the main building and the raised courtyard

11. Mezzanine plan of the ground floor

12. Ground floor plan

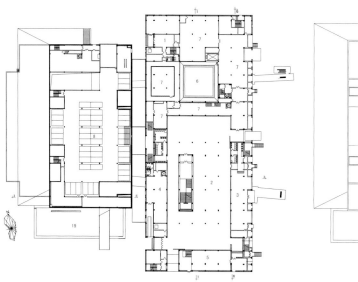

7

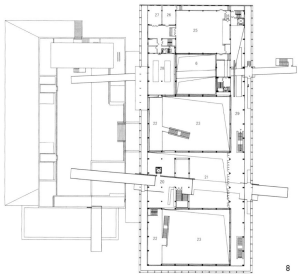

8

1 Doorway	8 Garage	14 VIP entrance	20 Doorway	26 Break room
2 Exhibit preparation area	9 Showroom	15 VIP reception	21 Lobby	27 Assembly room
3 Art salon	10 Doorway	16 Flat roof	22 Small showroom	28 Roof (air-conditioning)
4 Art bookstore	11 Training centre	17 Bar	23 Main showroom	29 Atrium
5 Gallery	12 Reception	18 Garden	24 Studio area	
6 Inner garden bamboo grove	13 Office area	19 Pond	25 Lecture hall	
7 Exhibit preparation area				

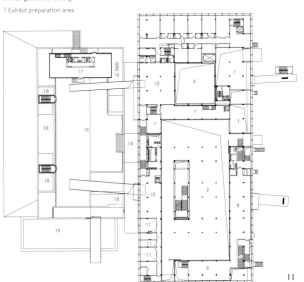

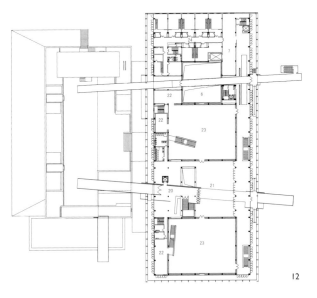

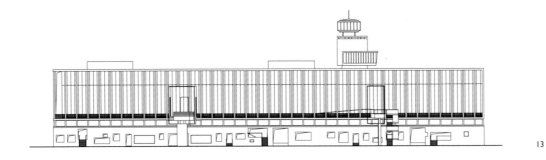

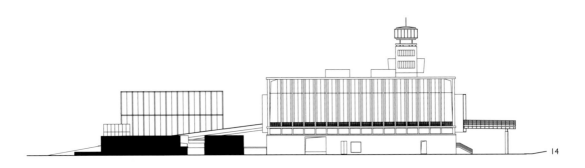

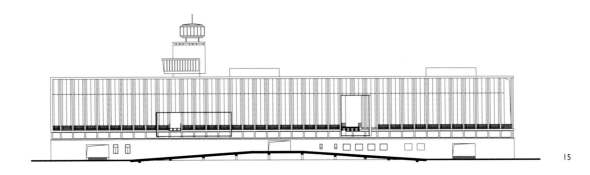

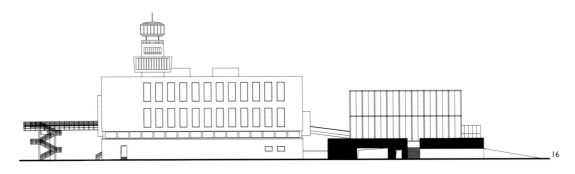

13. East elevation
14. South elevation
15. West elevation
16. North elevation
17. Courtyard view

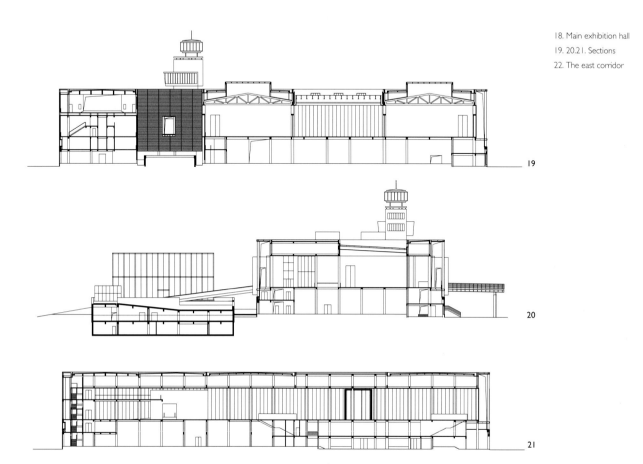

18. Main exhibition hall
19. 20.21. Sections
22. The east corridor

House A + B of Lushi Villa, Beijing

Architect: Wang Yun

Location: Lushi Villa, Shi Jing Mountain, Beijing
Design / Completion: 2003.03 / 2005.10
Area: Total area of House A: 838.97 sqm
　　　Total area of House B: 767.18 sqm
Architect: Wang Yun
Client: Real Estate Development Department of Beijing Construction Engineering Group

The Lushi Villa is located near Badachu in the Western Hill area of Beijing. Formerly the nursing resort of Beijing Construction Engineering Group, it covers an area of over 30,000 square metres and includes 52 two-floor villas. House A + B is a combination of two houses, which are named A and B respectively.

House A + B is the biggest villa in the resort, which has a total floor area (including the basement) of more than 800 square metres. The two houses each have their own inner and outer courtyards. The exterior courtyards are situated on the east side of the houses. Linked by two box structures 18 metres in length and width, and seven metres in height, the two houses comprise two floors above ground and one floor underground. On the east sides of the two houses, two courtyards 18 m x 12 m are positioned, from which there is a stairway leading to the basement. The interior space is a series of white boxes. This allows for an appreciation of the changing scenery outside as the viewer moves through the building.

The entrances of the two houses are simply scaled and designed. A long and slim pyramidal structure stands in front of the entrances with spotlights concealed behind, which is used for night lighting.

Houses A and B each have an unusual doorway. After entering the front door of House A, there is one more door, as well as a small sunken courtyard on the left, which brings sufficient sunlight into the interior space and serves as a light scoop for the basement. When entering the front door of House B, visitors must turn left to get inside. The living room of House B is a large, two-storey height space, with a French window only on the ground floor. Coming down the stairs from the first floor, visitors will enjoy a view of the whole living room. In this white and generous space, a small red door becomes the focal point. The living room of House A, when compared with the spacious inner courtyard, is less important in terms of the total volume of the house.

The master bedroom of House A is on the first floor, embracing

1. Distant view of House A + B from the central garden

an elegant curved wall among the unified linear structures. The master bedroom of House B overlooks the spacious living room and is fit for hosting a party. But it is positioned in a relatively hidden place, with windows facing the east to make the room bright.

The inner courtyard is linked with the outer by a grand staircase. What attracts visitors is that a long and narrow corridor with transparent walls connects the two. In House B, there is a square atrium with white walls, which is linked with the back garden through a long and narrow corridor.

All the furnishings are designed by the architect, and are made of various materials such as stainless steel, leather and plywood. The exterior walls are all in white, right-angled and bare, and they function as canvases for the changing light and shadow.

(All pictures supplied by the project architect.)

2

2. East courtyard of House A

3. Grand stairs connecting the terrace and the
courtyard of House A

4. East courtyard of House B

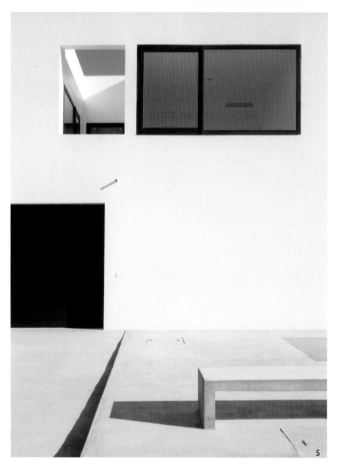

5

6

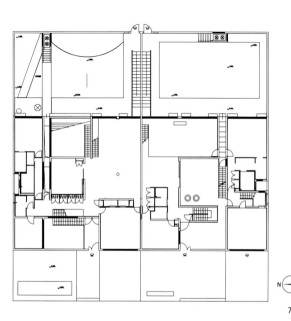

N

7

5. Connection between House A + B

6. Corridor on first floor of House A

7. Ground floor plan

8. 1st floor plan

9. Living room of House B

10. West elevation

11. East elevation

12. North elevation

13. South elevation

14. Section

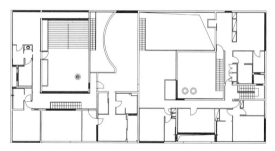

8

10

11

12

13

14

Well Hall, Lantian, Shaanxi

Architect: Ma Qingyun

Location: Lantian, Shaanxi Province
Design / Completion: 2005.4 / 2005.8
Area: 192.8 sqm
Architects: Ma Qingyun, Sun Daha, Wang Shan (M. A. D. A. Spam)
Client: Ma Qingyun´s father

1. Courtyard view

The Jade Valley Winery is located in the county of Lantian, southwest of Xi'an City, between the Qingling Mountain Range and the Guanzhong Loess Plateau. As the visitor centre for Jade Valley Winery, the Well Hall bridges indigenous style and a more exotic approach, evolving from the history and traditional culture of the area.

Situated on the top of a plateau, the Well Hall imitates the style of a house in the Guanzhong area, which features living rooms with small bay windows, wing-rooms with single-sloped roofs, and long, narrow courtyards. Based on these features, the architect makes some changes for the Well Hall with regard to the scale, materials used and new functions. With these changes, the building reflects the surrounding landscape context with its exotic flavour. The Well Hall, with the length extended and the wall made much higher, reflects the landscape of the surrounding mountains and rivers in scale. And consequently, its two courtyards appear much longer and narrower. The lower half of the

north wing-room is hidden in shadow, in sharp contrast to the other half that is exposed to bright sunlight. Under sunlight and shadow, these homogeneous materials show different textures and tones.

The brick outer walls of the Well Hall receive a special surface treatment. The two skin layers, inner bricks in red and outer bricks in grey, are "woven" together by interlaced header bricks. The grain of the rough wall surface and the resulting shadow effect moderates the height of the wall, making the building seem friendlier. This treatment is applied to the exterior wall only, while the two inner courtyards are partitioned by a simple brick wall. Therefore, it seems that the building is "wrapped" in the exterior surface. As result, the inner courtyards become external/internal spaces.

The building materials for the Well Hall are all from the local area. The builders are from neighbouring villages, and implement the construction according to MADA Spam's design sketch, remarks and hands-on demonstrations. During this process, emphasis has been

2. General view

3. 4. 5. 6. Details of the brickwork wall

7. Site plan sketch

8. 9. Sketches

placed on the specific site rather than the locality and indigenous style, which makes the building unique. On the one hand, the design concept is obtained from the local culture from a macro view; on the other hand, the Well Hall is constructed according to the specific site and functions from a micro view, which keeps it in harmony with the surrounding environment and village life.

(All pictures supplied by project architects.)

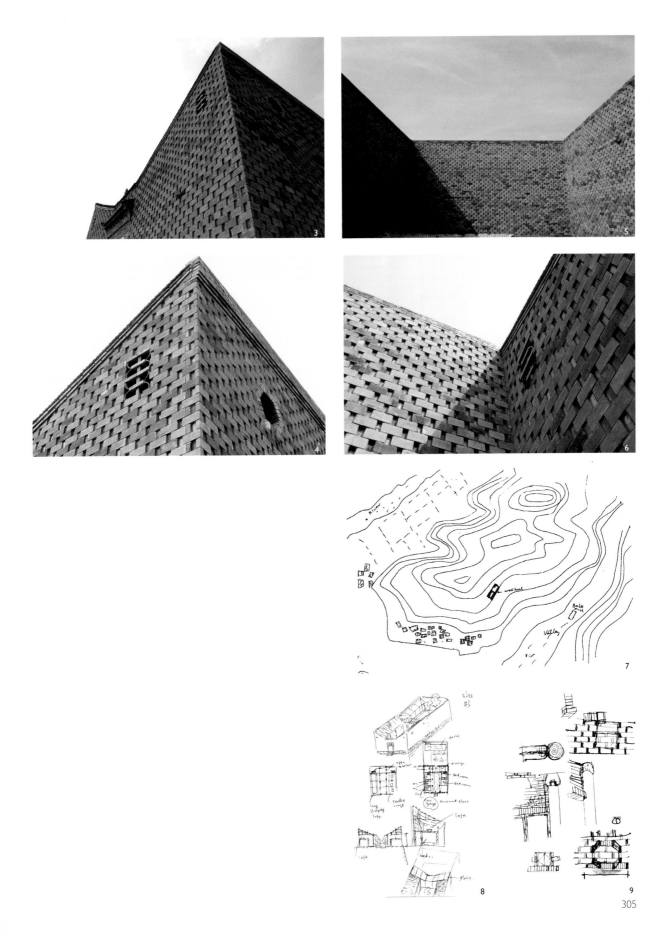

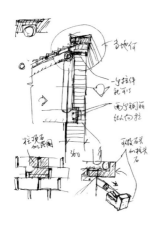

10.11. Partial view of the courtyard corridor

12. Window

13. Sketches

14. Courtyard view

13

14

The Apple Elementary School, Ali, Tibet

Architect: Wang Hui

Location: Ali, Tibet
Design / Completion: 2003.12 / 2005.08
Area: 1,850 sqm
Architects: Wang Hui, Dai Changjing
Client: Tarqing government (Contributed by Apple Foundation)

1. The view from the west

The Ali Apple Elementary School is located at the foot of the 4,800-metre high Kangrinpoche Mountain, a Buddhist shrine. It is the first completed project funded by the Apple Foundation and donated by the Antaeus Group.

Stones are prevalent in Tibet. Most buildings are constructed by piling up many large cobbles, without mortar. A lot of self-build cobble-concrete blocks are applied to the Ali Apple Elementary School. As the new building volume is homogeneous with the base in terms of materials, the two parts integrate well.

The cobbled wall along the slope, together with the buildings being scattered in groups, partitions the campus into many courtyards. The walls, arranged in a north–south direction, undulate just like the natural shape of the mountain. Due to the average of 149 windy days per year, one of the important functions of the walls is to keep off the wind. With reference to the local buildings in Tibet, the walls are placed in irregular shapes and at irregular intervals.

The buildings are arranged in groups, on the three bases and at different heights. This group arrangement reflects building formations in several villages within a 100-kilometre radius of the school. In addition this arrangement allows for construction to be carried out in different parts of the grounds at the same time, which shortens the total construction period. The buildings and walls in groups form different relationships between courtyards. These 20-plus courtyards, similar to each other but not identical, enrich the children's enjoyment of school life.

All the building units are south-facing, which makes full use of solar energy. By installing steel-framed double glazing and improving on the local solar energy system, the south wall is provided with functions such as lights, ventilation and heating. The indigenous solar energy system depends on a sort of corrugated iron, which is placed between double glazing. The iron is heated by the sunlight, and the resulting hot air heats the room when the interior glazing is opened. If

it is too hot, both layers of glazing are opened. The utilization of wind energy has also been taken into account. An equipment room for a wind turbine is included, which is small in scale and in similar in form to the other buildings.

The structure is designed to be as economical as possible, allowing for the local conditions. All the buildings are single-storey, which effectively reduces the difficulties in design and construction. In addition, the use of the fabricated in-situ cobble–concrete blocks is reduced, which cuts down the usage of concrete, making the building more cost-effective.

The cornices of the buildings are white, while the colours of the other parts are inspired by the traditional architecture of Tibet. The colour scheme is decided by teachers and students themselves according to their preferences. By selecting different colours, the local people have the chance to contribute their own ideas to the buildings they use.

The topography formed by piling up cobbles becomes a multi-functional landscape, which can be used as part of the playground, a place for children's outdoor activities such as reading and relaxing, or as a venue for the flag-raising ceremony.

(All pictures supplied by project architects. Photographers: Wang Hui, Cao Youtao, Yang Yang.)

2. The courtyards and walls

3. Site plan

4. Longitudinal section

2.400

1.200

1.200

1.200

±0.000

道路

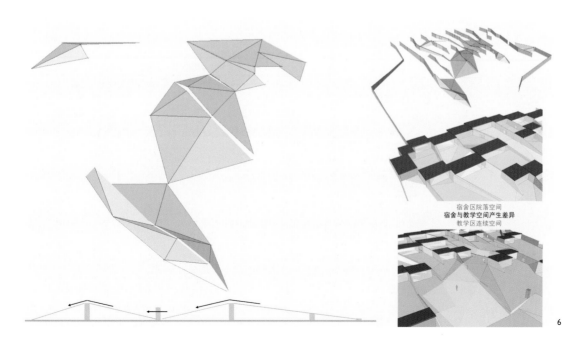

宿舍区院落空间
宿舍与教学空间产生差异
教学区连续空间

6

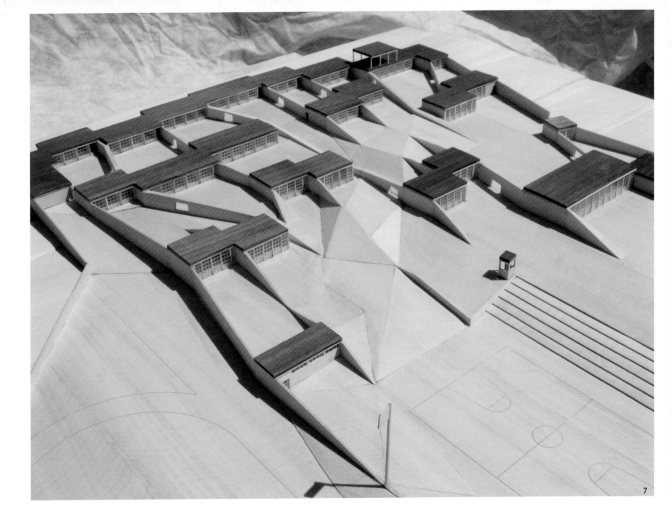

7

8

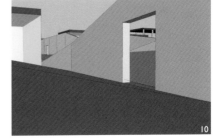

9

10

5. Courtyard
6. Topography analysis
7. Model
8. Perspective rendering
9. Spatial analysis 1
10. Spatial analysis 2

12

13

11.12. Framed view of the courtyard

13. The courtyard under the blue sky

14. Toilet

Huacun "Project Hope" Elementary School, Deyang, Sichuan

Architects: Zhu Tao, Li Shuqing

Location: Tongshan Town, Zhongjiang County, Deyang, Sichuan Province

Design / Completion: 2004.03-2004.04/ 2004.10-2005.07

Area: 1,350 sqm

Architects: Zhu Tao, Li Shuqing, Deng Jing, Xu Yunchao

Client: Shanghai Qingshan Huacun Inc.

1. Exterior view, Huacun "Project Hope" Elementary School

The project is located in Tongshan County in Sichuan Province in southwest China, a poor and isolated mountain region, yet one with a breathtakingly beautiful landscape.

Equipped with 12 standard classrooms and four offices, this new elementary school is intended to replace the existing one within the County Central Elementary & Middle School Campus, which is adjacent to the site and in a run-down condition.

The architects proposed an L-shaped building with two wings, each of which sits on a different ground level, so as to both preserve the existing contours on-site and formulate a new courtyard as an extension of the existing school complex, characterized by the inner courtyard layout typical of the area.

The single-loaded corridors of the two wings all face the courtyard, which has a gentle slope. The architects insisted on making certain areas of the corridors unusually wide (3.5 metres), despite the fact that typical school corridors in China are much narrower. These generous areas allow for students' casual social gatherings and fun-filled moments between classes. Especially with the local rainy climate, these extra-wide corridors become essential on rainy days for students' daily activities outside their classrooms. Following the natural topography, various platforms, stairs and steps are arranged around the building all over the site to encourage children's outdoor activities.

The architects strived to maximize the use of natural light and natural ventilation throughout the building. The top floors of classrooms have clerestory windows up high so that natural light can penetrate deep into the classrooms. A series of vertical light/ ventilation openings was made in corridor floors as well as their roofs adjacent to the classroom walls, to bring daylight down to the lower floor and to increase the natural air flow.

A tight budget is the dominant constrain of this project. This rendered the project automatically in the category of "regionalism"; its feasibility and realization relied heavily on using local, common

materials. Yet, the architects still strived to generate vitality out of the harsh constraints.

In the preliminary study, the architects attempted to explore a roof in the shape of a three-dimensional folded surface built in steel, to initiate a dialogue with the traditional two-dimensional pitched roof in timber construction that is omnipresent in the surrounding vernacular houses and the existing school complex. With further development, they differentiated the roof-work in two ways: the traditional two-dimensional pitched roof covered with clay tiles for the even, repetitive and cellular units of classrooms and offices; the three-dimensional folded-surface roof covered with corrugated metal panels (later replaced by corrugated asbestos panels) for the corridors as a response to the inherent spatial dynamics and the surrounding undulating topography.

In contrast to the floating roof-form, the main body of the building, built of brick walls and concrete slabs, with a strong feeling of "corporeality", is anchored deeply in the ground.

(All pictures supplied by project architects.)

2. Mixed structure of the roof truss

3. Mixed structure of wood roof truss supported by steel columns

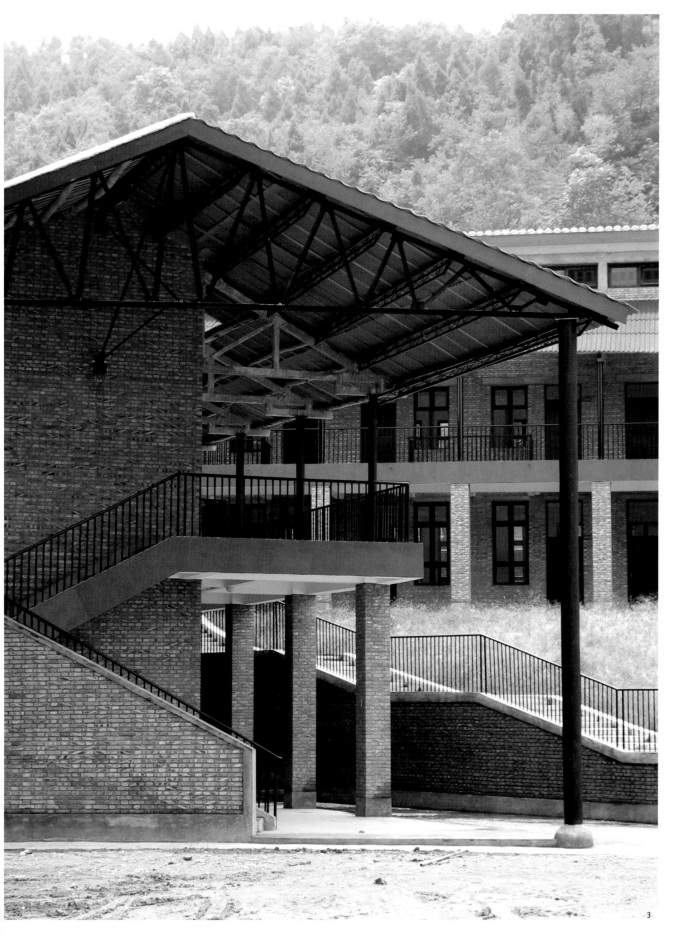

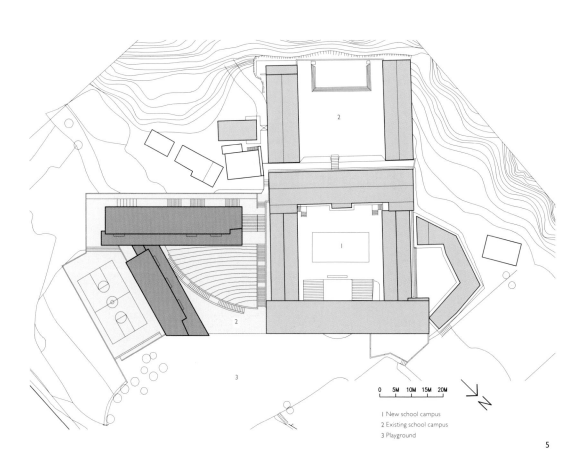

0   5M   10M   15M   20M

1 New school campus
2 Existing school campus
3 Playground

5

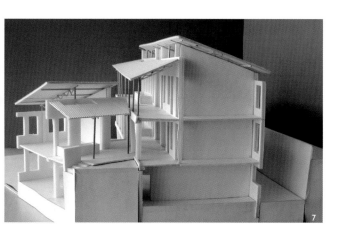

4. 6. 7. 8. Models

5. Site plan

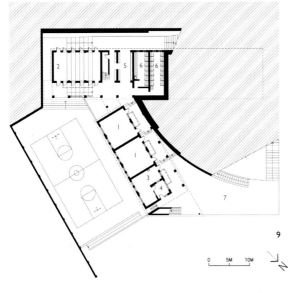

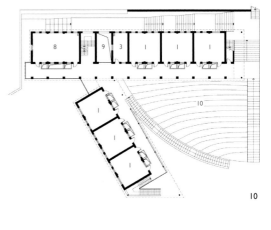

9

0 5M 10M

1 Common classroom   7 Entrance square
2 Theatre   8 Multi-functional classroom
3 Teachers' office   9 Hall
4 Transmitting room   10 Turfed slope
5 Hall   11 Roofing
6 Toilets

10

11

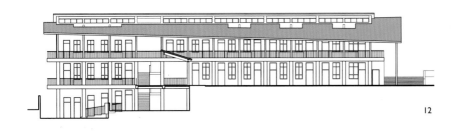

12

13

9. Ground floor plan
10. 1st floor plan
11. 2nd floor plan
12.13. Elevations

15

15. Detail of mixed structure roof truss

16. Section

17. Outside corridor

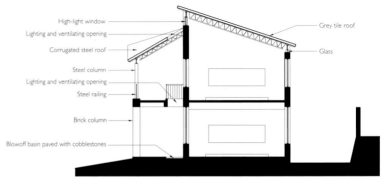

High-light window

Lighting and ventilating opening

Corrugated steel roof

Steel column

Lighting and ventilating opening

Steel railing

Brick column

Blowoff basin paved with cobblestones

Grey tile roof

Glass

16

Office Building for Qingpu Private Enterprise Association, Shanghai

Architect: Atelier Deshaus

Location: Qinglong Rd, Qingpu New Town, Shanghai
Design / Completion: 2003-2004.10 / 2005
Area: 6,745 sqm
Architect: Atelier Deshaus
Client: Qingpu Private Enterprise Association

1. Southeast view

Located on the east side of Xiayang Lake in the new area of Qingpu District, the office building belongs to the Xaiyang Lake Landscape Area. In order to create a relationship with Xaiyang Lake, the location of the cube-shaped structure responds to its axis. The site was once desolate, but is now covered in grass.

The architects took into consideration the views not only from the interior but also from the exterior. The solution is a cube covered with a glass curtain wall. The cube building is 60 m x 60 m. The three-storey glass wall encloses a green yard that creates a boundary offset from the building by at least four metres. The clear glass wall appears to dissolve the boundary. While obviously defining the private space in the interior, the transparent glass also creates a visual communication between the landscapes inside and outside. The main buildings are arranged in a square shape with a courtyard at the centre. The first floor is elevated and only houses the reception and a restaurant. In this way, the ground floor spaces flow from the central garden to the exterior landscape and there is an uninterrupted view through the building. The construction of this office building was part of the larger urban planning, therefore, to stay in harmony with the surroundings, the architects designed a strip of bamboo garden in between the glass walls and the inner main buildings. These open the inside up to the surroundings and at the same time provide privacy.

The glass walls work as a boundary, and create a microclimate in this area. Firstly, they largely reduced the noise from the highway to the east. In Chinese gardens, the ponds and trees in a courtyard are the significant factors in creating a microclimate. During the summer, the vapour from the pond with the elevated floor provides a circulation of air that reduces the temperature inside the building. When a visitor goes into the building, the sudden cooling effect from the garden brings a feeling of serenity.

Glass panels hang on the façade with stainless steel fixings, fixing the glass at the right, left and the bottom. Each panel has a gap

between it and the next. The architects screen-printed the curtain glass wall of the inner main structure. This gives a wholeness to the visual form, and also works as a shading system. The pattern of screen-printing chosen is a pattern inspired by "broken ice" and the image of a dragonfly's wings.

In the interior design, the architects used white as the dominant colour; white artificial stone, white paint on the metal trussed roof, as well as glass and timber. The impression on entering the building is of a calm and inspiring atmosphere.

(All pictures supplied by project architects.)

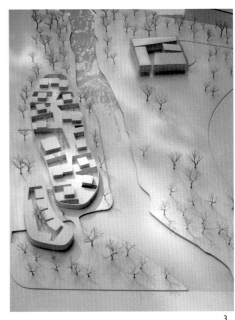

3

2. North view
3. Model
4. Site plan
5. Partial view of the elevated area

4

5

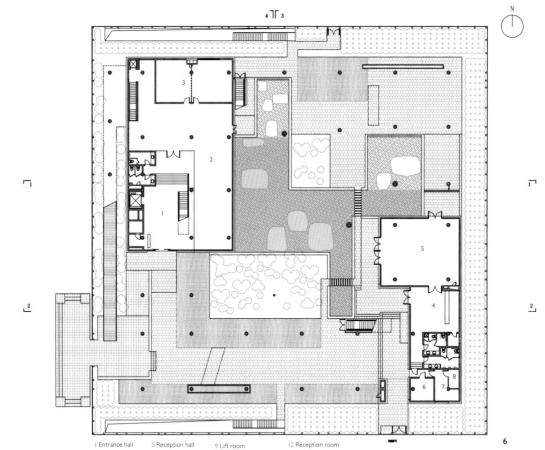

N

1 Entrance hall	5 Reception hall	9 Lift room	12 Reception room
2 Dining room	6 Fire control	10 Office	13 Staircase
3 Chartered room	7 Duty	11 Assembly room	14 Break room
4 Service room	8 Telephone room		15 Atrium

6

7

6. 5. Ground floor plan

7. 1st floor plan

8. Terrace for the entrance
to the 1st floor

8

9. Terrace for the entrance to the 1st floor
10. North elevation
11. West elevation

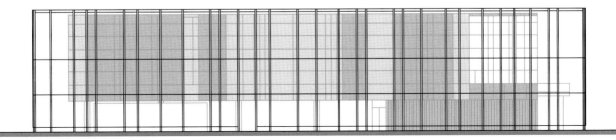

10

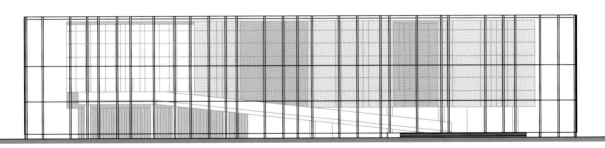

11

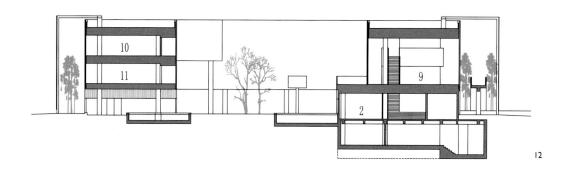

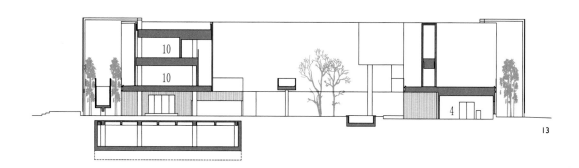

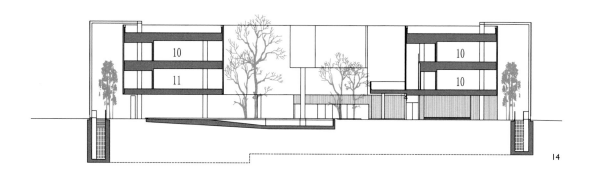

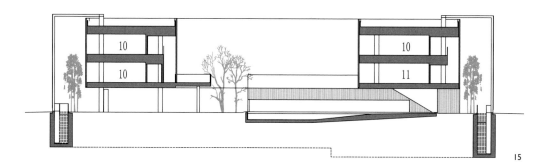

12. 13. 14. 15. Sections

16. Interior view

17. Night view of the courtyard
18. Printed glazed curtain wall
19. Exterior view of curtain wall

MBA Centre, Nankai University, Tianjin

Architects: Zhou Kai, Xu Qiang

Location: Nankai University, Tianjin
Area: 29,388 sqm
Design / Completion: 2001 / 2005
Architects: Zhou Kai, Xu Qiang
Client: Nankai University

1. Exterior views of the roof garden

Nankai University is one of the first nine pilot schools for the Master of Business Administration (MBA) programme. Its MBA Centre, belonging to the Business School of Nankai University, was established as the administrative office for MBA education in July, 1999. The teaching and administrative building for the MBA Centre was completed in 2005.

The MBA Centre building is located on the campus of Nankai University to the east of Baidi Road, Nankai District. Being west of the Baidi Road, next to the west entrance of Nankai University, south of the apartment building for postdoctoral researchers of Nankai University and east of the Xuefu Garden villa area, it is provided with a favourable location. The centre covers an area of 8,260 square metres, which seems narrow compared with the 30,000 square metres of construction area allowed. The building lies symmetrically along the axis that is parallel to the Baidi Road.

The MBA Centre building contains mainly four kinds of functional

spaces, which include, ranked in size: multi-functional lecture halls, multi-media classrooms open to the public, standard classrooms, and offices and discussion rooms for lecturers and doctoral candidates. Besides their different requirements for location, orientation and height, these four types of functional space are required to be arranged in a particular way.

As one of the school buildings, the budget for the construction is not great. Therefore the design should be practical and integrated, eschewing frivolous decoration. Situated on the ground floor, the entrance hall and multi-functional halls are clad in black stone and form a plain, dark base, on top of which sit two white cuboids. The concave shape of the building is turned into a square by four pre-stressed concrete pillars. Clad in pre-stressed concrete panels in a wood-like colour, the multi-media classroom is embedded in the white cuboids, which not only satisfies the lighting requirement, but also solves the problem of the inconsistent façade due to the differing

storey heights. The office space lies in the concave part to the west. To provide shelter from the direct rays of the sunset and in the cut openings of the façade, a 1.2-metre wide balcony is positioned. A grey fence lines the veranda, which makes the building façade appear as a homogenous whole.

The project attempts to create an academic atmosphere by providing places such as a high wall, outside staircase, roof garden and courtyard, to promote the environmental quality of the building. Being close to the busy road, the west entrance connects with the front garden, which not only lessens the effect of the road, but also highlights the entry. The grille sunshade over the front garden casts shadows on the side wall, which, together with the green bamboo, creates a peaceful atmosphere. To disperse crowd flow, there are stairs on both sides of the lecture hall. From the stairs, the lecture hall can be accessed from different levels. The stairs go from the front garden to the roof garden above the lecture hall, lined by the high

walls in deep grey. The bamboo casts shadows on the wall, adding to the overall feeling of peace and serenity.

(All pictures supplied by project architects. Photographer: Wei Gang for Fig 1-3, 5; Zhou Kai for Fig 9, 11 and Yang Chaoying for Fig 12.)

2

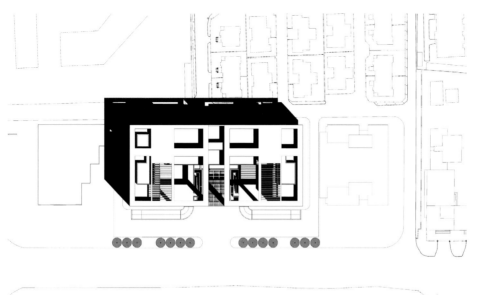

2. Northwest view
3. Details of the lobby
4. Site plan
5. Model

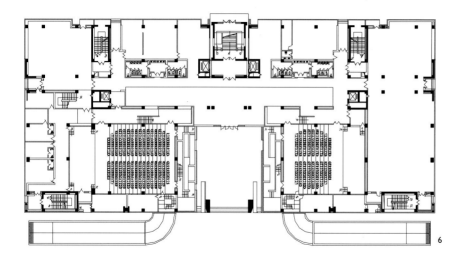

6. Ground floor plan
7. Mezzanine plan
8. 1st floor plan
9. Exterior views of roof garden

6

7

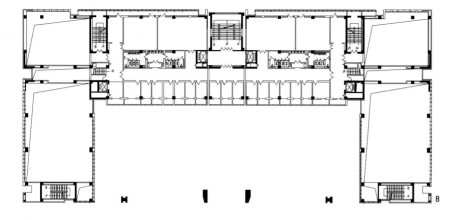

8

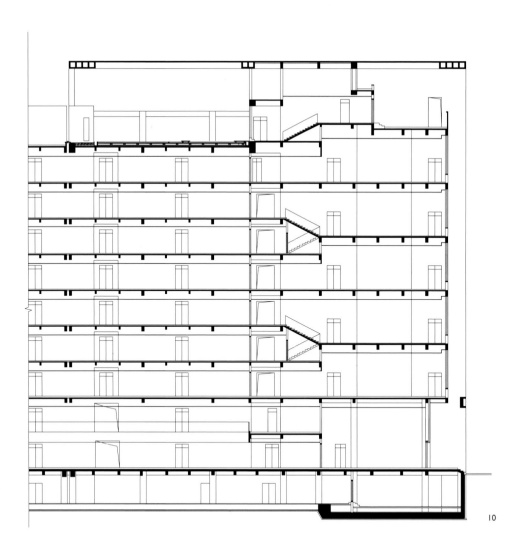

10

11

10. Section

11. Exterior view of roof garden

12. Entrance garden

13. West elevation

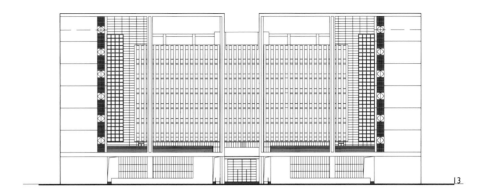

Dalinor National Natural Reserve Tourist Orientation Centre, Inner Mongolia

Architect: Zhang Yonghe

Location: Dalinor National Natural Reserve, Inner Mongolia, China
Design / Completion: 2003 / 2005
Area: 1,500 sqm
Architects: Zhang Yonghe, Feng Guoan, Wang Hui, Yu Lu, Dai Changjing, Yang Chao
Client: Canadian Agricultural Consultation, Ltd., Dalinor Goverment

In Mongolian, "Dali" means sea, and "Nor" means lake, so "Dalinor" means a sea-like lake. The Dalinor Lake lies in Khaskatun Qi, Chifeng, Inner Mongolia. To the north is the remote Gongge'er prairie, and to the south is the boundless Hunshandake Desert. In this area, there are diversified grassland habitats, peculiar scenes of woodland in sandy land, lakes and marshes inhabited by all kinds of birds, and the well-preserved paleo-volcanic mesa physiognomy. Being an important passage in north China for bird migration as well as a main habitat for migratory birds, it has been classified as a national natural reserve. Besides receiving tourists and students, the Tourist Orientation Centre also introduces the reserve and popularizes environmental protection knowledge, especially about migratory birds. The building of the centre, known as the "bird-observation deck" by local people, was jointly completed by local government and an environmental protection institution from Canada.

This single building is of moderate scale, 50 metres long, 20 metres wide and less than five metres high. It is sited, in an east–west direction, about 1,000 metres to the north of the lake, with only one level above ground and most of the rest underground. The roof partly consists of sloping ground that the centre is built into. The ground part, except for the glazed exterior wall on the east side and the wall at the entrance, is covered with turf, which makes the site, the exterior wall and the roof one natural and continuous surface. The bird-observation deck includes several terraces composed of green "flagstones" (or rigid grass-planted platforms) and ramps, and each can be accessed from three directions. Tourists can get onto the deck from almost all directions to view the building and the surrounding landscape. On the south side there is a sunken square with the backdrop of Dalinor Lake. With big steps at either end that can be used for relaxation or displaying exhibits, the square seems to be available for outdoor performances or exhibitions. The ramps, together with the platforms and sunken courtyard, soften the edges

and the base of the building, and seem to reach out to the prairie beyond. In harmony with the surrounding environment, the building looks as if it was born from the prairie.

Inside the building, the spaces are divided into a reception area, offices, exhibition area and projection room, which are connected by steps and ramps. The glass panels and metal balustrades around the flat roof did not exist in the concept drawing, but were deemed necessary for safety.

The building appears as part of the natural environment of the prairie. Sitting beside the Dalinor Lake, listening to the songs of swans, you may find that the outline of the centre has already melted away into the background.

(All pictures supplied by project architects. Photographer: Liu Yang.)

1. South elevation and the nearby volcano
2. Site plan

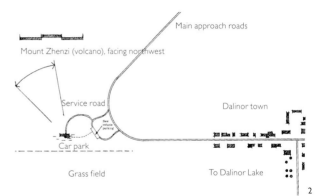

Mount Zhenzi (volcano), facing northwest

Main approach roads

Service road

Dalinor town

Car park

Grass field

To Dalinor Lake

3. The ramp up to the roof

4. The north side and the entrance

5. Ground floor plan

6. Roof plan

7. Lower ground floor plan

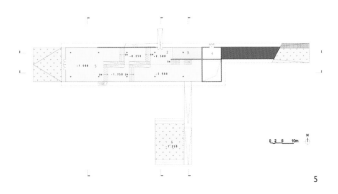

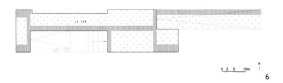

1 Entrance
2 Entrance lobby
3 Reception
4 Service room
5 Exhibition area
6 Outdoor theatre
7 Toilets
8 Storage
9 Projection room
10 Projection preparation room
11 Wooden observation deck

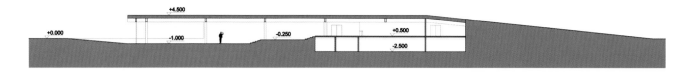

9

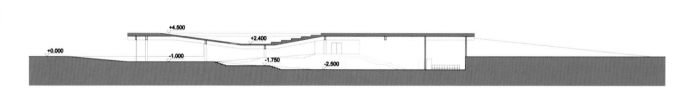

0 2 5   10m

10

15

16

8. Southwest of the exhibition area

9. 10. Sections

11. Distant view

12.13. Outdoor theatre and the ramp to
the exhibition area

14. Northwest of the exhibition area

15. 16. 17. Sections

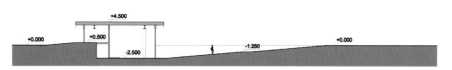

17

0 2 5 10m

Construction Regulatory Centre of Qingpu New Town, Shanghai

Architect: Liu Jiakun

Location: Qingpu District, Shanghai, China

Completion: 2005

Area: 10,155 sqm

Architect: Liu Jiakun

Client: Construction Regulatory Centre of Qingpu New Town

Client: Qingpu Private Enterprise Association

1. East facade

The Construction Regulatory Centre of Qingpu New Town is designed on the basis of the dialogue about "Minimum" and "Maximum". A black cuboid structure, it stands upright aside the Qingpu Museum, fully occupying the long and narrow base by using the simplest structure. In an interpretation of this context, the Qingpu Museum, shaped like a white magnolia flower, lies in a big green space, while the centre is designed in a natural and low-profile style. The 190-metre long structure makes full use of the maximum area of the base, which seems huge and impressive to visitors. There are many upright blinds, which accentuate the east–west direction of the façade. The 0.6-metre space between blinds contrasts with the 190-metre length of the whole building; the bulky stone seats at the entry, the cascading parterre and the stones on feature walls can be interpreted as an artistic conception by viewers, encouraging them to contrast the details with the whole; the minimum with the maximum.

While the functions and the users of the building had not been determined by the government during the planning phase, the users now include: "Qingpu New Town Construction and Development Group Co., Ltd" in the northern ground floor, "Qingpu Urban Planning Exhibition Hall" in the continuous large space on the southern ground floor, "Qingpu Planning Administration Bureau" on the first and the second floors (see plans). As Liu Jiakun said, to some extent, the building had been re-built three times before it was finally completed. The storeys increased from two to three, and a two-storey high atrium space was made in addition to the flat and enclosed space. Considering the special requirements for spaces and functions, the architect focused on the adaptability of the space and the flexibility of the functional arrangements. With regard to functional arrangements, the building is divided into two parts: the upper is for administrative offices, the lower is for exhibition space. Though divided into three levels, its spatial structure and mode of access are very simple.

Encircled by a pool, the ground-floor entrance looks light and peaceful. Three yards are surrounded by grass which adjoins the exhibition hall on the ground floor. Looking from the pool, the vision is partially hindered by densely covered stone blinds, which creates a mysterious atmosphere. In the interior spaces, the multi-functional exhibition hall seems randomly partitioned, which implies the possibility of change in the future. According to the actual needs of the area, the big functional space can be flexibly divided into smaller spaces, which provides more options for practical uses. The first and second floors are reserved for offices and meeting rooms. By the same logic as above, the big functional space can be divided into large or small spaces at will. The external flat roof is connected to the ground-floor yards by an external staircase, which provides views of and contrasts between the upper and lower levels.

When approaching the Construction Regulatory Centre of Qingpu New Town, viewers will be no doubt deeply impressed by the care and attention paid to the detailing of the architecture. Grey-black stones, laid with the narrow side outwards, create a strong feature wall at the entrance. The unpolished sides of the stones are visible, and look exquisite, lyrical and impressive. The 600 mm x 600 mm one-piece black stone seats at the entrance of the Qingpu New Town Development Centre, with polished faces and hewn sides, are placed in series, which makes the entrance platform above the pool appear solid and strong. The design of the stone blinds of the façade looks more creative when observed closely. Black stone slats, spaced 600 mm apart, 450 mm long and 35 mm thick are repeatedly placed facing outwards. There are three types of slats classified by height: 1350, 1200 and 850 mm, which are set up at different intervals according to their height. To be fixed stably, a 15-mm steel plate is embedded inside the window frame. The stone slats themselves are finely processed: the narrow side is hewn to be rough and protuberant, and the wide side, pre-polished, is incised

every 20 mm to form grooves that are 5 mm in width and depth. Every finely made slat can be regarded as an artwork. These stone blinds can not only be used as sun shading, but also diffuse the indirectly reflected light into the interior space. A transparent curtain wall is placed in the space between the first floor and the second floor in order to collect light. The pure and delicate transparency of the wall contrasts with the massive texture of the stone blinds. Compared to the landscape and lighting conditions faced by the south façade, the other three sides of the building are faced only by roads and car parks. Accordingly, all these sides are covered by stone walls that are inlaid with glass windows. According to the different lighting needs, the architect sets up the windows at irregular intervals. By doing so, the building's mass is highlighted, and its dignified and benign appearance is heightened.

It is not the attractive interior space but the control of the exterior form that dominates the design of the Construction Regulatory Centre of Qingpu New Town. Freely employing the materials, Liu Jiakun has his own insights into the context of the areas south of the Yangtze River. The creative, exquisite and decent sense of the form as a whole is what makes his language; the grey-black colour shows power even in a low-profile building, while his critical thinking about repetitive building techniques embodies the building's value with respect to contemporary art.

(All pictures supplied by project architect. Photographer: Lü Hengzhong, Yuan Feng, Zhi Wenjun.)

2. Overview

3. South facade

4. East plaza

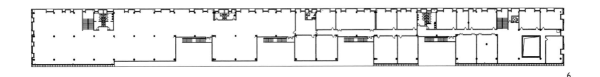

6

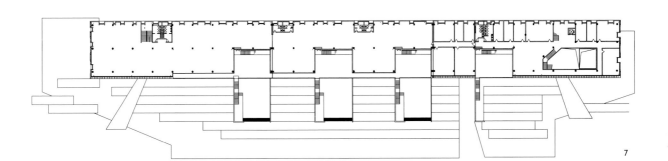

7

5. External view

6. 2nd floor plan

7. 1st floor plan

8. 9. 10. 11. Details

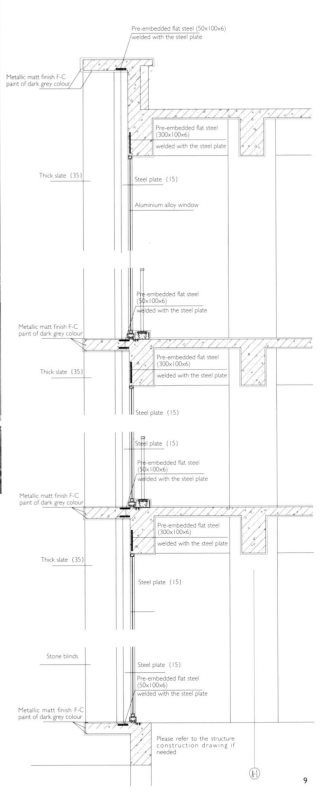

Pre-embedded flat steel (50×100×6) welded with the steel plate

Metallic matt finish F-C paint of dark grey colour

Pre-embedded flat steel (300×100×6) welded with the steel plate

Thick slate (35)

Steel plate (15)

Aluminium alloy window

Pre-embedded flat steel (50×100×6) welded with the steel plate

Metallic matt finish F-C paint of dark grey colour

Pre-embedded flat steel (300×100×6) welded with the steel plate

Thick slate (35)

Steel plate (15)

Steel plate (15)

Pre-embedded flat steel (50×100×6) welded with the steel plate

Metallic matt finish F-C paint of dark grey colour

Pre-embedded flat steel (300×100×6) welded with the steel plate

Thick slate (35)

Steel plate (15)

Stone blinds

Steel plate (15)

Pre-embedded flat steel (50×100×6) welded with the steel plate

Metallic matt finish F-C paint of dark grey colour

Please refer to the structure construction drawing if needed

9

New Jiangwan Ecological Exhibition Centre, Shanghai

Architect: Miao Pu

Location: Luohu District, Shenzhen

Completion: 2004 / 2005.05

Area: 3,620 sqm

Architects: Miao Pu with Shanghai Landscape Architecture Design Institute

Client: Shanghai Chengtou Corporation

On the north edge of Shanghai, an isolated wetland of about 10 hectares has remained undisturbed for several decades. Now it has become a nature reserve and a part of the park system of New Jiangwan City, a new town developed around the wetland. Since the reserve cannot allow everyone to enter, it is necessary to establish an exhibition/observation centre on its west side for the public to use. In the architect's long-term plan, two elevated walkways will radiate from the centre into the reserve so that the entire area will be accessible to the public.

Two concepts govern the building design. First, the architect broke away from the "black box" stereotype of museum design, making live species and the outdoor natural environment the main exhibits. On the first floor, a semi-underwater window nearly 13 metres long shows sections of the wetland at various depths (to be completed when the water system of the reserve is rehabilitated). Five cameras are installed across the reserve. Visitors can see real-time images anywhere in the reserve by directing a laser pointer at the corresponding area of a model on the ground floor. The sunken courtyard outside the west wall on the first floor displays, through a window, typical plants in the wetland. Finally, the observation deck on the roof afford visitors a direct, panoramic view of the wetland. A cantilevered observation deck extends 7.5 metres into the wetland to allow visitors a closer look of the tree-tops and birds.

Secondly, the architect also borrowed the idea of "gradual revelation" from traditional Chinese architecture to create a sense of mystery so that visitors will treasure the reserve even more. To people on the street the building appears as a small hill with many trees, blocking views further into the reserve. After walking downwards into the half-buried ground floor, visitors are attracted to the underwater window, which makes people temporarily forget what happens above the water's surface. On the first floor, a layer of metal mesh with ivy hangs outside the glass wall facing the reserve.

1. Main entrance and lift/stair tower emerging from the hill

In addition, a layer of film is glued onto the glass wall to show historic maps of Jiangwan. Only after the visitors climb onto the roof deck, does the scenery of the reserve fully reveal itself to them. People can then return to the entry plaza through a path on the slope of the man-made hill.

The architect imagined the building as a little "submarine" anchored at the wetland. People in the boat can observe nature through underwater, electronic and panoramic "eyes". With its west side buried in a planted hill and its east elevation and roof trellises to be covered by climbing plants in a few years, the green building will merge naturally into the wildness of the reserve.

(All pictures supplied by project architects.)

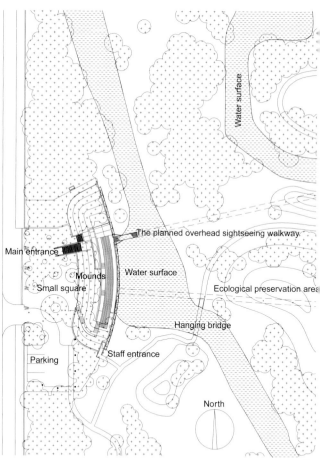

The planned overhead sightseeing walkway

Main entrance

Water surface

Mounds

Small square

Ecological preservation area

Hanging bridge

Parking

Staff entrance

North

2. Shady, downstairs entrance suggests entering "another world"
3. Site plan
4. From the entrance looking towards the underwater windows in the ground-floor exhibition hall

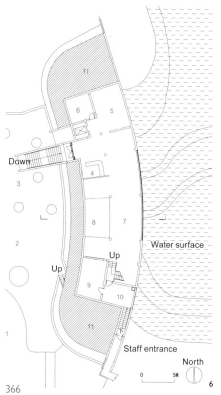

Down

3

2

Up

Up

6

5

4

8   7

9

10

11

Water surface

Staff entrance

North

0   5M

6

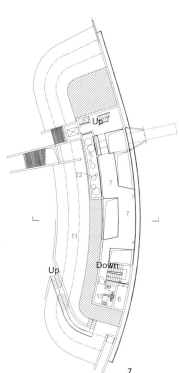

Up

12

11

7

7

Up   Down

13   6

7

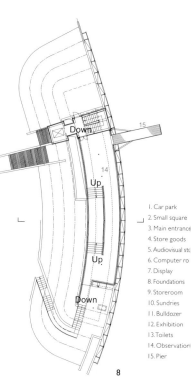

Down

15

14

Up

Up

Down

8

1. Car park
2. Small square
3. Main entrance
4. Store goods
5. Audiovisual st[c]
6. Computer ro[om]
7. Display
8. Foundations
9. Storeroom
10. Sundries
11. Bulldozer
12. Exhibition
13. Toilets
14. Observation
15. Pier

5. The observation decks on the roof

6. Basement plan

7. 1st floor plan

8. Roof plan

9. The cantilevered deck in the east elevation

10. Section

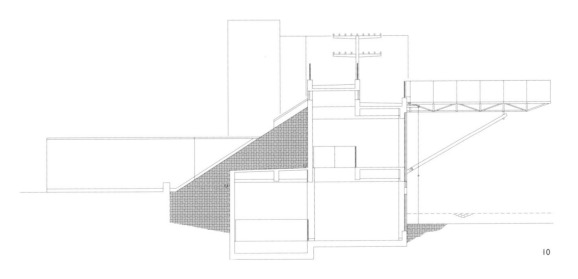

10

Wuhan CRI and French–Chinese Arts Centre, Wuchang

Architect: Standard Architecture

Location: Wuchang
Design / Completion: 2004 / 2005
Area: 1,500 sqm
Architects: Zhang Ke, Zhang Hong, Hao Zengrui, Han Xiaowei,
Yang Xinrong, Liu Xinjie, Li Linna, Jing Jie, Lin Lei, Han Liping
Client: China Resources Land Ltd

The site of the arts centre is located across the street from the Wuchang Tanhualin historic area, about one mile away from the historic Huanghelou Tower on the Yangtze River. The expectation was that the building would be an important public space for the city and a monument both for the past and for the ongoing transformation of the city. The fact that many famous Chinese intellectuals lived in the Tanhualin area across the street inspired the architects. They were interested in testing the possibilities of building something out of the ancient Chinese intellectual practice of ink-and-water. The arts centre was conceived as an urban container, within which art objects, events, acts, concepts and activities flourish. In this case the container is made out of intuitive images of ink-and-water.

The site conditions also take part in the formation of spaces: since the site is cut in half by unexpected urban infrastructure (a flood pipeline), the 30-metre-wide outdoor space became the central courtyard for spatial organization. Around it sit the east and west exhibition halls and the floating bridge linking the two parts. In the 80-metre-long concrete bridge, the ink-water stroke texture coincides with the necessary structural elements for the 5.5-metre-high concrete hollow beam. This creates an interesting moment – when an image merges seamlessly with a structure.

(All pictures supplied by project architects. Photographer: Cheng Su.)

1. Southwest view of the centre from along the street

2. Model viewed from southwest corner

3. Site plan

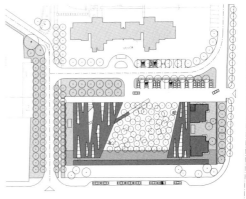

4. Ink-water texture projected inside the corridor

5. Ink-water sketch for the floating corridor

6. South view of the centre along the street

7. Ink-water sketch for roof plan of the west hall

8. Skylights and structural plan

9. Waterside platform between the west hall and the floating corridor

10. Interior view of the floating corridor

11. Section of the west hall and the floating corridor

12. Exterior view of the floating corridor

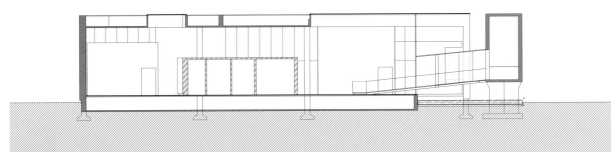

12

13. Multi-media space floating inside the west hall
14. East hall viewed from the ramp leading to the floating corridor

15. Containers of various functions inside the west hall
16. A quiet area inside the exhibition hall

The Yangshuo Storefronts, Guilin

Architect: Standard Architecture

Location: Yangshuo, Guilin
Design / Completion: 2003 / 2005
Area: 7,000 sqm
Architects: Zhang Ke, Zhang Hong, Claudia Taborda, Qi Honghai,
Wang Wenxiang, Liang Hua, Han Xiaowei, Qin Ying, Hao Zengrui,
Liu Xinjie, Yang Ying, Du Xiaomin, Gai Xudong
Client: Sunshine 100

This small neighbourhood is built on a block of 2,300 square metres and comprises five small alleys and six separate buildings. The buildings occupy the entire boundary of the site, and the main alleys inside work as continuations of the neighbouring urban fabric. The architects found a way to have the main alleys point towards the major mountains nearby, namely the Lotus and the Dragon Head Mountains. As a result of this layout, all the six buildings became irregular in plan. On the ground floor there are small shops and the shop owners live on the first floor. There are corridors linking all the buildings on the second and third floors. Units on these floors each have a bathroom and a kitchen. They could function either as apartments or as shops. Passing through the bridges linking each building, people will always find special views towards the surrounding karst mountains.

The neighbourhood is built mainly from four local materials: the blue-greenish Yangshuo stone, larch-wood panels, small grey tiles and bamboo strips. The "city control regulations" supposedly ask for all the buildings to be painted white, but the architects discovered that this was not actually the case. The local villages never have large areas of white-washed walls – they are all bult from exposed local stone and grey bricks.

Seen from a distance, the storefronts have nothing startling about them. But when coming closer, most people will be surprised by the appearance of the central building. Bamboo strips six metres long and six centimetres wide are placed at eight-centimetre distances from each other, at right angles to the building façade. Behind this bamboo layer, there is a layer of folding wood panels. When the wood panels are opened, the people inside could have the sense that there is only a curtain of bamboo strips separating them from the karst mountains.

(All pictures supplied by project architects. Photographer: Chen Shuo.)

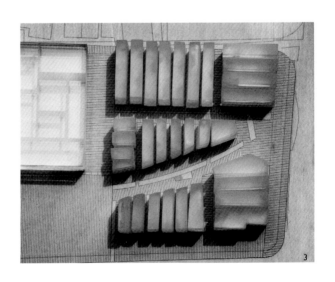

4

2. Model of Yangshuo

3. Concept model

4. Corridor and the second floor bridge

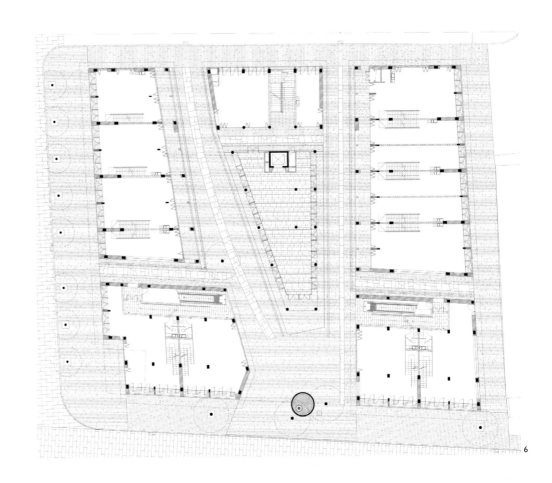

5. Entrance plaza
6. Plan
7. Third floor bridge

8

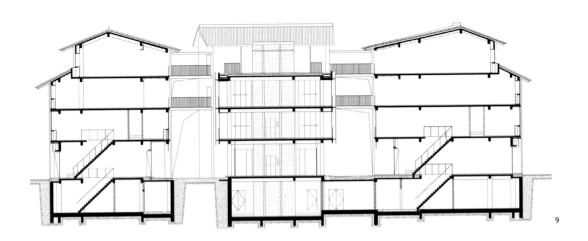

9

8. View of main street towards Mount Dragon Head

9.11. Sections

10. Bamboo hall and colonnade

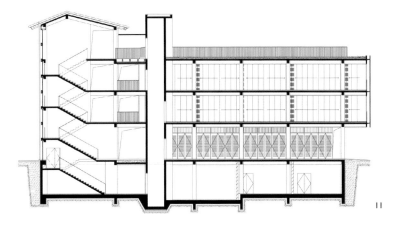

12

12. View of the bamboo facade from the elevated path

13. Partial exterior view

14. Facade of bamboo strips

15. Detail of dry stone wall in Yangshuo

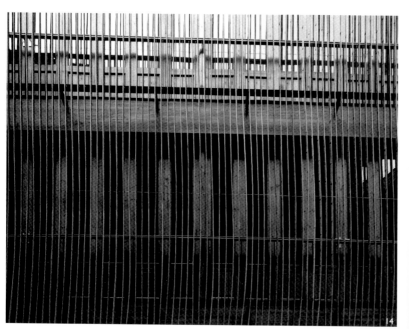

Xiangshan Campus, China Academy of Art, Hangzhou

Architect: Wang Shu

Location: Xiangshan, Zhuangtang, Hangzhou, Zhejiang Province
Design / Completion: Phase I 2001 / 2004
                Phase II 2004 / 2007
Area: Phase I 70,000 sqm
      Phase II 78,000 sqm
Architects: Wang Shu; Lu Wenyu; The Amateur Architecture Studio;
Contemporary Architecture Creation Study Centre, China Academy of Art
Client: China Acadamy of Art

1. Overview of Xiangshan Campus Phase I

The new campus of the China Academy of Art is located near Xiangshan Mountain, Hangzhou. The masterplan of its Phase I project is a morphological simulation of the natural relationships between mountains. Ten building units imply the formation of the mountains, in association with the former villages on the site. The Phase I project, which was designed in 2001 and completed in 2004, is occupied by the Public Art Institute, the Media and Animation Institute, a library and a gymnasium.

The Xiangshan Campus, which is built in a mixed pattern of traditional academy and learning garden, embraces various structural styles: cloisters as you would find in an abbey, a combination of the Renaissance master's workshop and the modern studio, a Bauhaus-style workshop, as the symbol of elementary education on modern art, structured as an enclosed pedestal for all building units, and even scattered and disordered sites like the practice grounds in Buddhist Cave Temples. These diverse structures all fit in with the

changeable landscape surrounding them. The concealed nature of the site highlights the dedication to quality of education and the campus environment. The buildings on the site tend to hide themselves, as a metaphor for the art education hiding behind the landscape after making its contribution. The Xiangshan Phase I project is partitioned by courtyards with openings facing the mountain at different angles. The angles, openings and locations are precisely defined. Based on the partitions, the form and the detail of the units are adjusted accordingly to interpret the relationship between the site and the scene. The phase II project at the south of the Xiangshan hill was designed in 2004 and completed in 2007, and consists of ten large buildings and two small ones. It contains the School of Architectural Art, the School of Design, an art gallery, a gymnasium, the students' residential building and a dining hall. The new buildings are all arranged around the edges of the site. Between the buildings and the hill, a large space is left empty, in which the original farm, river and

ground are preserved. The form of each building evolves naturally along with the undulation of Xiangshan Hill.

On the campus, the building plans appear as if arranged by accident; space feels vacant or compact, public or private; two elevations may be very different in the one building; all of this results in a series of locations in which events happen quickly. There is no strict structure, allowing for everyday life to happen easily. This is the understanding of the traditional Chinese garden, which is especially expressed in the Phase II project at the south of Xiangshan.

Similarly to the Phase I project, the land beside the buildings and roads is re-leased to the farmers, on which to plant crops. Land tax will not be charged. A 200-metre long water channel connects the land to the river and runs across the campus, which is not only regarded as a beautiful addition to the landscape, but also supplies the field and the pond with water.

The structure consists of a reinforced concrete frame, steel in some parts, and brick walls, which are common in the local area. By using a lot of low-cost recycled bricks and tiles, and taking full advantage of local construction methods, the local masonry of multi-size bricks and modern architectural techniques are integrated, to create a thick wall system that is thermally insulated. This not only saves resources, but also makes a great impact on the ecological consciousness of teachers and students.

As with Phase I, the Phase II project to the south of Xiangshan takes a period of 14 months to complete. Many problems, which come from the handwork used during the construction process, are solved by working on-site. After input by so many people, the building was given a sense of its own, unique "life".

(All pictures supplied by project architects. Photographer: Lü Hengzhong.)

2

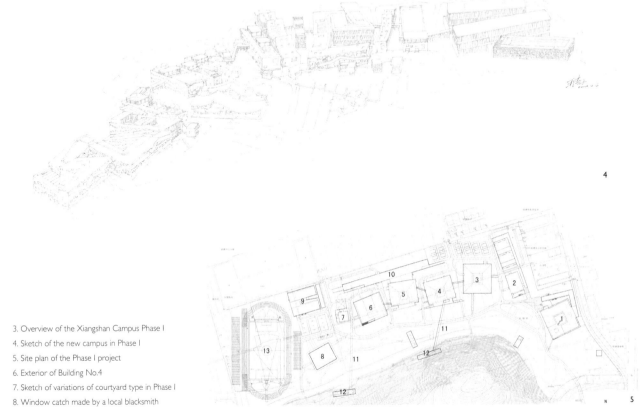

3. Overview of the Xiangshan Campus Phase I

4. Sketch of the new campus in Phase I

5. Site plan of the Phase I project

6. Exterior of Building No.4

7. Sketch of variations of courtyard type in Phase I

8. Window catch made by a local blacksmith

6

7

8

9. View including landscape
10. Ground floor plan of Building No.2
11 1st floor plan of Building No.2
12. Roof plan of Building No.2
13. 14. Elevations of Building No.2
15. Section of Building No.2

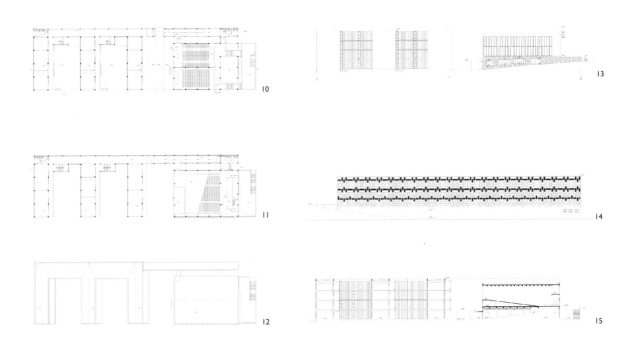

底层平面（Ground floor）

层平面（First floor）

顶层平面（Roof plan）

Re-1a轴立面（Re-1a elevation）

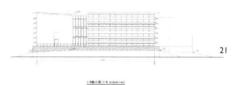

1-8轴立面（1-8 elevation）

B-B剖面图（B-B section）

A-A剖面图（A-A section）

16. Neighbourhood and context
17. Ground floor plan of Building No.1
18. 1st floor plan of Building No.1
19. Roof plan of Building No.1
20. 21. Elevations of Building No.1
22. 23. Sections of Building No.1

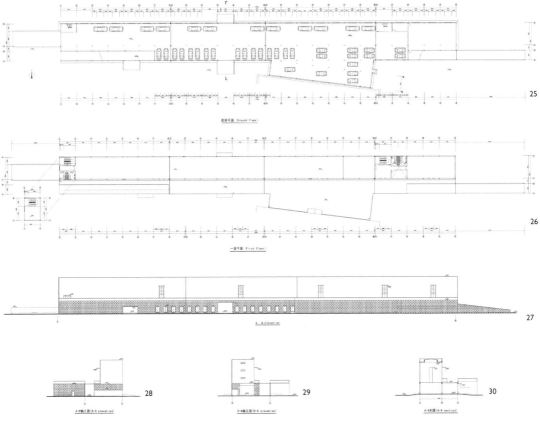

底層平面 (Ground floor)

一層平面 (First floor)

G-G軸立面 (G-G elevation)

A-O軸立面 (A-O elevation)

D-A軸立面 (D-A elevation)

A-A剖面 (A-A section)

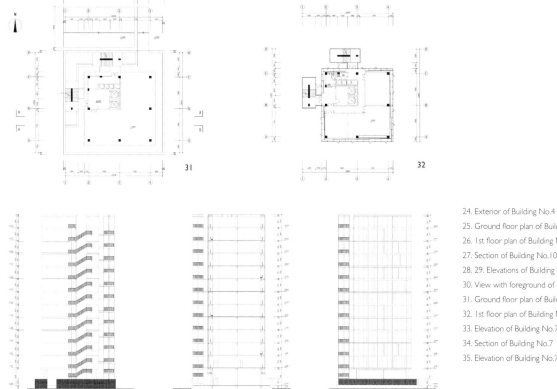

24. Exterior of Building No.4

25. Ground floor plan of Building No.10

26. 1st floor plan of Building No.10

27. Section of Building No.10

28. 29. Elevations of Building No.10

30. View with foreground of Building No.7

31. Ground floor plan of Building No.7

32. 1st floor plan of Building No.7

33. Elevation of Building No.7

34. Section of Building No.7

35. Elevation of Building No.7

36. West view of Building No.11

37. Site plan of Phase II, Xiangshan Campus

38. Ground plan of Building No. 11

SITE PLAN

36

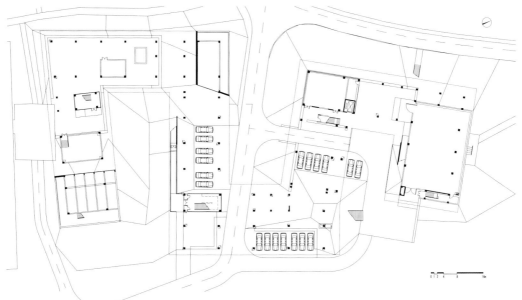

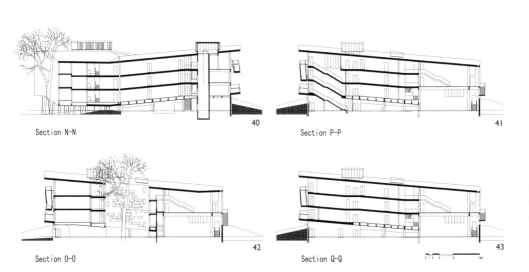

Section N-N 40

Section P-P 41

Section O-O 42

Section Q-Q 43

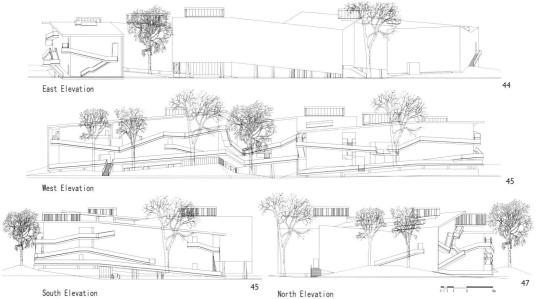

East Elevation 44

West Elevation 45

South Elevation 45

North Elevation 47

48

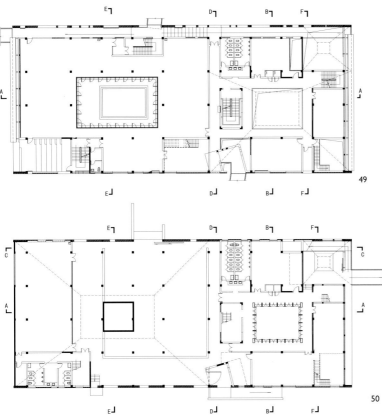

49

50

North Elevation

South Elevation

58

59

57. Courtyard of Building No. 13

58. Patterned window of Building No. 13

59. Staircase of Building No. 13

60. 1st floor plan of Building No. 13

61. 62. Elevations of Building No. 13

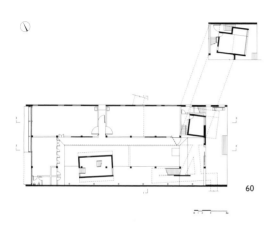

60

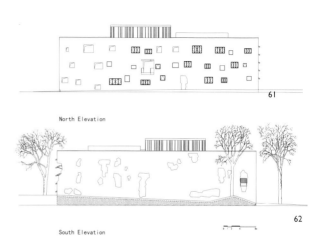

61

North Elevation

62

South Elevation

63. Courtyard view of Building No.14
64. 1st floor plan of Building No.14
65. Courtyard view of Building No.14

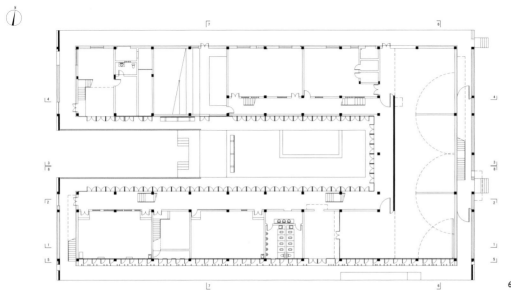

64

66. Perspective view of Building No.14
67. 68. Sections of Building No.14
69. 70. Elevations of Building No.14

Section 1-1

67

68

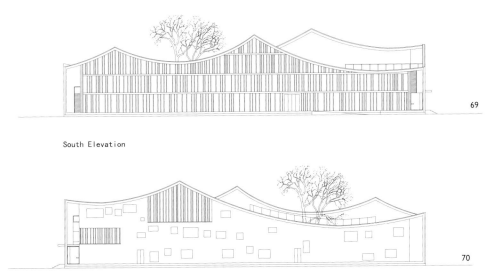

South Elevation

69

70

71

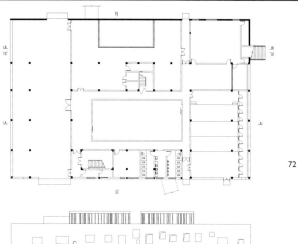

72

71. Northwest view of Building No.15 at night
72. 1st floor plan of Building No.15
73. 74. Elevations of Building No.15
75. 76. Sections of Building No.15
77. Courtyard of Building No.18
78. South elevation of Building No.18

73

North Elevation

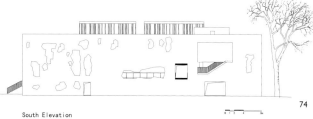

74

South Elevation

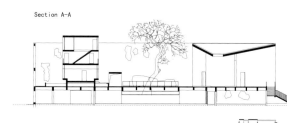

75

Section A-A

76

Section B-B

77

78

79. Overview of Building No.19
80. 2nd floor plan of Building No.19
81. Night view of Building No.19
82. 83. 84. 85. Sections of Building No.19

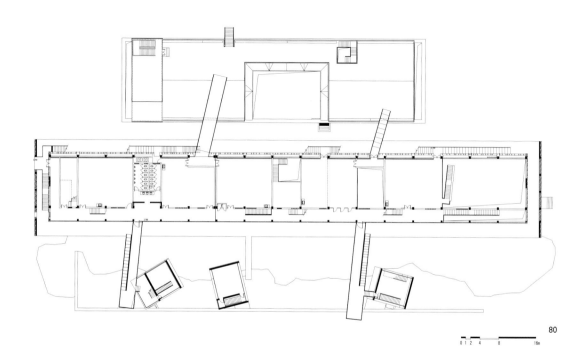

0 1 2 4   8   16m

80

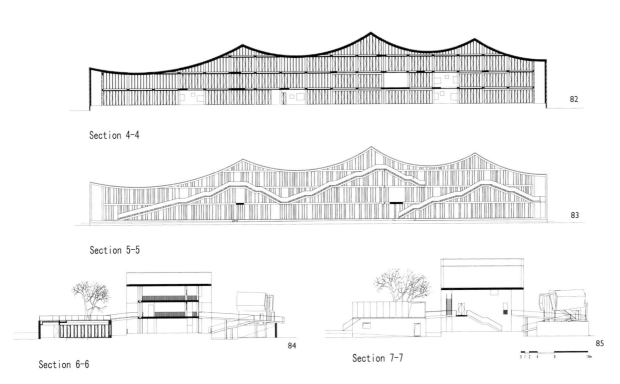

Section 4-4

Section 5-5

Section 6-6

Section 7-7

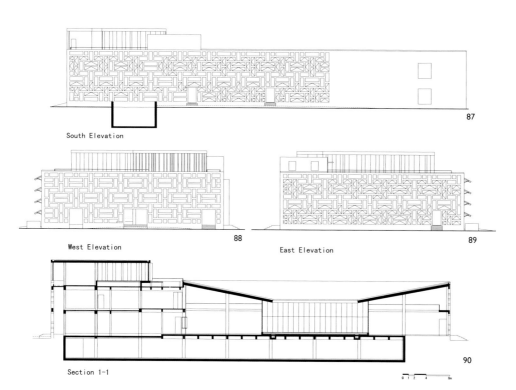

South Elevation

West Elevation

East Elevation

Section 1-1

86. Roof-top view of Building No. 21
87. 88. 89. Elevations of Building No. 21
90. Section of Building No. 21
91. Interior view of Building No. 21

Xiayu Kindergarten, Qingpu, Shanghai

Architects: Atelier Deshaus

Location: Hua-Le Road, Qingpu New Town, Shanghai
Design / Completion: 2003-2004 / 2004.11
Area: 6,328 sqm
Architects: Atelier Deshaus
Client: Qingpu District Government

Xiayu Kindergarten lies on the edges of the Qingpu New Town. Qingpu is one of the several sub-districts around Shanghai, and still preserves some traditional buildings. Since Qingpu New Town was basically built up from farmland and it is far away from the old town, Xiayu Kindergarten can hardly be influenced by the style of local traditional buildings. In fact, the area around the site is vacant; thus the traditional urban feeling is non-existent. The elevated highway on the eastern side is a potential source of exhaust gas and noise, but it also provides the possibilities of viewing the building from various angles. The river provides a more pleasant landscape, but also demands thought about the children's security and the form of the building by the river.

In the design of Xiayu Kindergarten, the architects emphasized the difference between inside and outside. They moderately isolated the inside and outside of the building by emphasizing the boundary, thereby creating a stark difference between them. The inner region is entirely protected, while the outer environment is filtered.

The kindergarten contains 15 classes, and each one has its own living room, dining room, bedroom and outdoor playground. After placing all the functions in a linear arrangement along the narrow site, the architects found that a soft, curved form would suit the site better than a straight line. The 15 classrooms and teacher offices were separated into two curve-clusters that are wrapped by solid and void materials respectively. A painted wall delineates all the classrooms, while the offices and special classrooms are enclosed by glazing.

In the design of the class units, the architects arranged all the living rooms on the ground floor with outdoor playgrounds, and left brilliant coloured bedroom boxes on the first floor. To emphasize the floating and uncertain feeling they detached the coloured boxes' floors from the roofs of the ground floor. This uncertainty and isolation leads to a seemingly random convergence and produces

1. View from northwest

spatial tension. Every third bedroom is linked by a raised wooden walkway, thus creating a friendly and kind atmosphere, like a "bedroom village".

Architectural volumes are scattered among the tall trees dotted in the courtyards. Thus the architecture and the tall trees bring out the best in each other and cohabit harmoniously on the narrow riverside.

(All pictures supplied by project architects. Photographer: Zhang Siye.)

2. West facade facing the river

3. Model

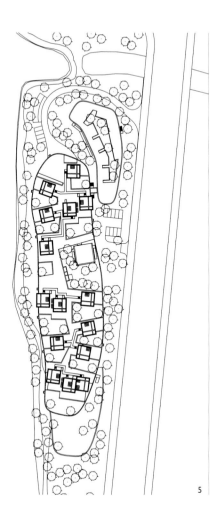

4. View from the east

5. Ground floor plan

6. 1st floor plan

7.8. Views of exterior space

9.10. Views of courtyard space

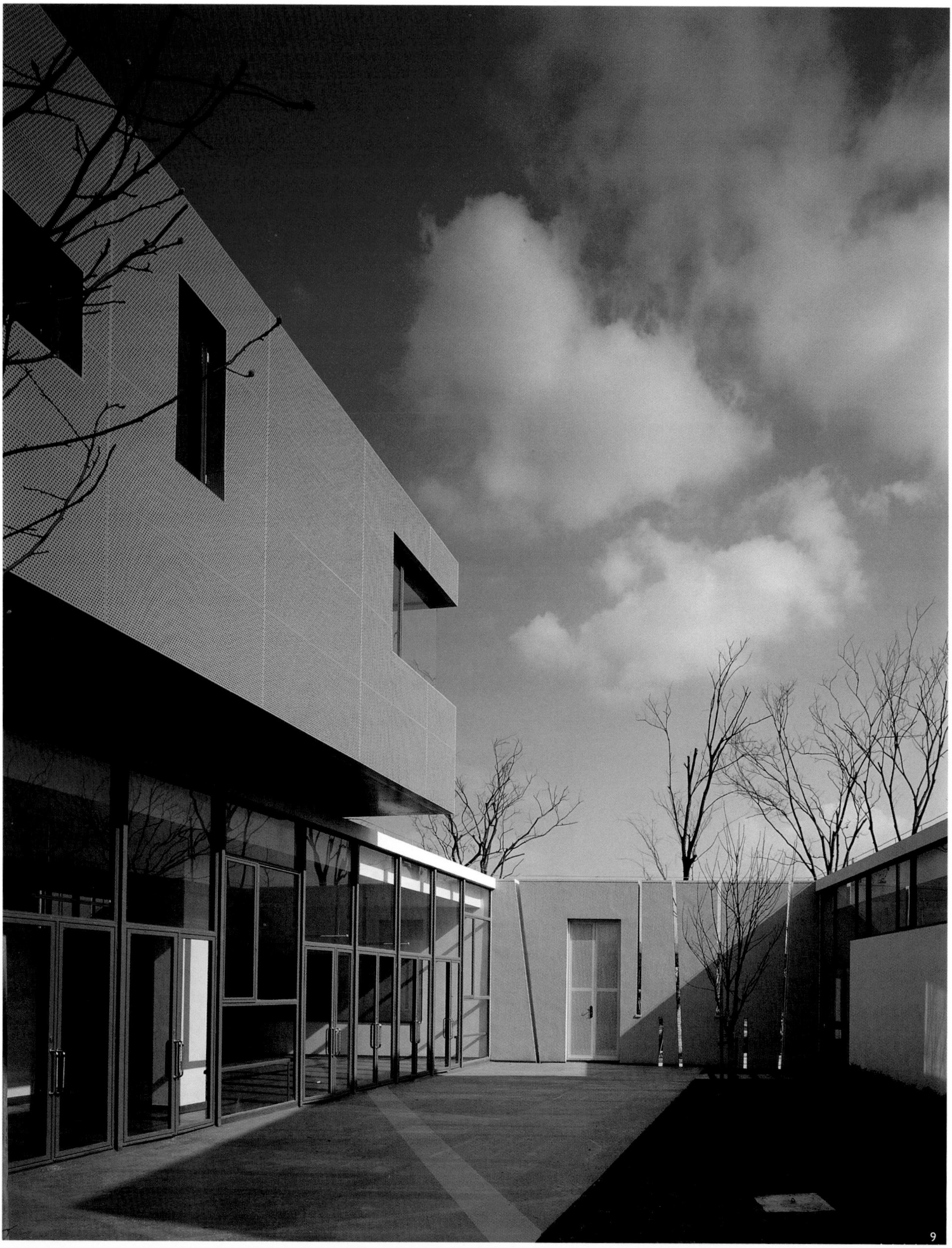

11. View from the northwest

12. East elevation

13. Part of west façade

14.15. Views of interior corridor space

The Main Museum and the French Museum at Fuping Pottery Art Village, Xi'an

Architect: Liu Kecheng

Location: Fuping Pottery Art Village, 1 Qiaoshan Road, Fuping, Shaanxi
Province
Design / Completion: 2004. 01 / 2004. 08
Area: 1,600 sqm
Architects: Liu Kecheng, Fu Qiang, Xu Dongming, Fan Chunfei
Client: Xu Dufeng, Fu Qiang (Fu To Industries)

1. Interior view of the Main Museum (Photographer: Dong Ke.)

The Fuping Pottery Art Village was completed in 1998, and is about 70 kilometres away from the north of Xi'an. It belongs to a private enterprise called "FUTO Ceramic Industrial Group". At the location there was formerly a tile factory; now there is a group of buildings including hotels, studios, museums and galleries. The museums are to the northwest of the orchard and adjacent to the pottery factory. The round pottery workshops, with flat-arched roofs, are situated on the edge of the orchard. The Main Museum, inaugurated in 2004, is at the northwest corner of the orchard, while near the entrance of the orchard is the French Museum, inaugurated in 2005. Both of them were designed by Liu Kecheng.

The architectural language in the Main Museum makes reference to forms of ceramic art. Based on the analogical elements in these forms, the design also draws inspiration from observations of the firing kiln and empty interior spaces of pottery forms. The structural elements reflect this also: the arched-ceiling main gallery stands on the ground, with two parallel galleries that look like two ceramic pots lying next to it.

The arched-ceiling structure is of great significance. On the one hand, it draws inspiration from the traditional building system of local buildings – the arched brick ceiling. On the other hand, in order to fit the wavelike form of the roof of each gallery, an irregular arched-ceiling system is set up, which consists of piles of arches reinforced by a concrete structure that is sometimes exposed.

The general layout illustrates the links between the three main parts. The two parallel galleries are set up a few metres away from each other, and are connected through a flat-roofed space with little height. From these two galleries, people can go into the arched-ceiling main gallery through a passageway, most of which is invisible from the outside. When viewing the whole site, people can clearly discern the links between each part of the museum. The museum is coloured matt grey by the concrete coating, which ensures the unity

426

2. Exterior view of the Main Museum (Photographer: Liu Kecheng.)

3. Model of the Main Museum (Photographer: Xu Dongming.)

4. Sketch by Liu Kecheng

5. Site plan of FuLe International Ceramic Art Museum

of the whole building. On the approach to the museum, a few tombs in a simple style remind us that the site has a historical relationship with local villages.

The French Museum is in a rectangular form facing the arched-ceiling roof of the Main Museum, but at a distance. This arrangement reminds us of the configuration of the kiln in ceramic crafts, which is often set up on a gentle slope to enhance heat circulation. In this landscape, the building with its simple geometric form stands in a low position on the horizon. The uniform impression comes from the sombre tone of the main building, which is caused by the brick facing that covers the wall and the flat roofs leaning against the wall. The brick facing consists of a few interlaced patterns in brown and chocolate colours.

The façade facing the entrance of the orchard is composed of square, rectangular and trapezoidal elements, which are sometimes placed at a slant. They are placed on the ground, and divided into two parts. The partition is established by a stone parapet wall a few metres in front of the building, which seems to extend into the building. When looking from a distance, this gives the effect of depth, and strengthens the impression of the axiality of the middle part of the building. The centrality of the façade is established by the precise distribution of the true and the false. Through the viewing window people can see part of the interior space. The entrance is inconspicuous, and people enter the museum through a dim porch.

(All pictures supplied by project architects.)

428

4

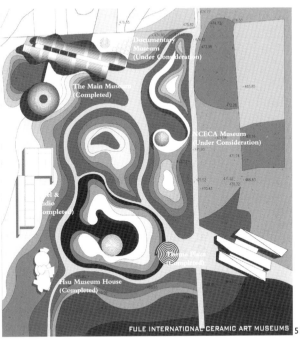

FULE INTERNATIONAL CERAMIC ART MUSEUMS 5

Documentary Museum
(Under Consideration)

The Main Museum
(Completed)

NCECA Museum
(Under Consideration)

Hotel &
Studio
(Completed)

Hsu Museum House
(Completed)

Taoma Plaza
(Completed)

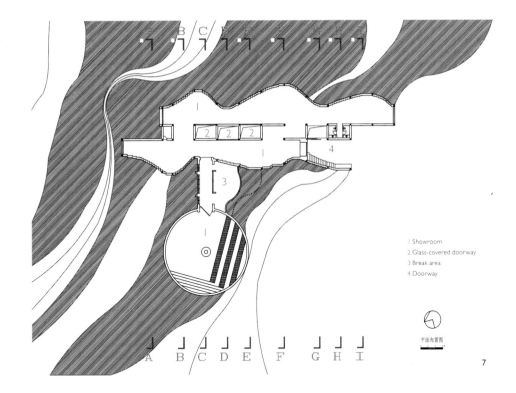

1 Showroom
2 Glass-covered doorway
3 Break area
4 Doorway

平面布置图

7

9. Interior view of the gallery

10. East view of the Main Museum (Photographer: Dong Ke.)

11. Fuping Folk Ceramic Art Exhibition on show in the Main Museum. The focus of the exhibition is work by Ms Wang Biyun, the artist in residence of Fuping Pottery Art Village, who transplants her experience of making "dough flowers" into pottery. (Photographer: Dong Ke.)

12. Sections and elevations

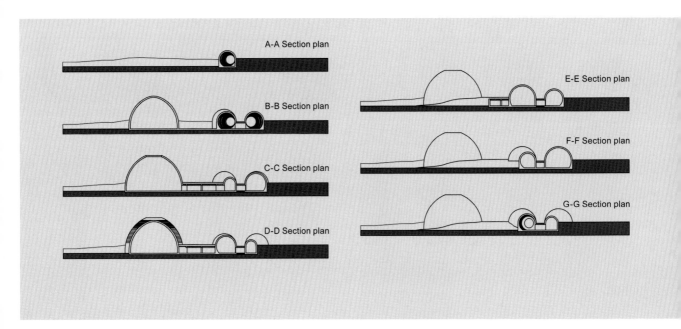

13

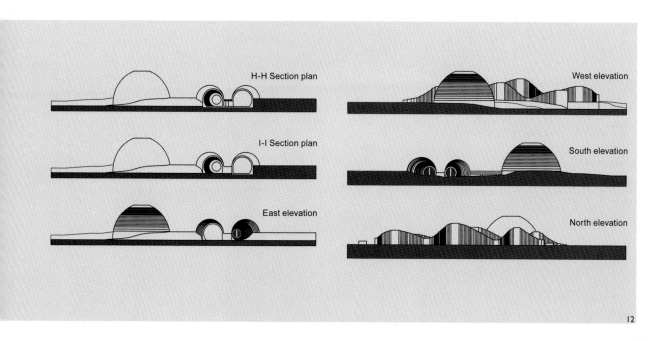

H-H Section plan

I-I Section plan

East elevation

West elevation

South elevation

North elevation

12

13. Exhibits in the top-lit courtyard

14. Entrance

15. Interior view of the dome, Main Museum

16. Exterior view of the French Museum

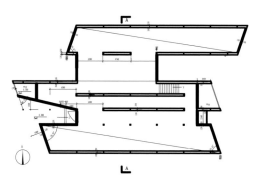

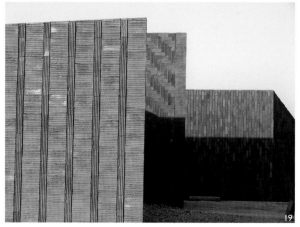

17. East facade of the French Museum, where a low wall stretches out as a signifier of the dividing of different levels of the galleries

18. Plan, French Museum

19. The cladding of the French Museum - ceramic tiles produced by Fu To Industries

20. The skylight brings contrast to the galleries within the French Museum

Building C of CAUP, Tongji University, Shanghai

Architects: Zhang Bin, Zhou Wei

Location: Principal Campus of Tongji University, 1239 Siping Road, Shanghai
Design / Completion: 2002. 02 / 2004. 05
Area: 9,672 sqm
Architects: Zhang Bin, Zhou Wei
Client: Tongji University

1. View from southeast

As an extension to the main building of CAUP (the College of Architecture and Urban Planning), Building C is programmed for research and graduate student education on a congested site, with the main building adjoining on its western side and the campus enclosing wall on its northern side. The appearance of this building is intended to reveal the dormant potential of this silent corner in the campus, and to re-establish its relationship with the campus, the main building and the city. This is a building that needs to encourage communication and inspire hidden enthusiasms and creative instincts, and in this way the process of using it is also the revelation of dormant potential in the users themselves. The space is envisioned as a kind of flowing continuum and the rigid relationship between service and serviced space is broken down, so that the communication space becomes the main component, and the functional space is a "plug and play" element. The core of Building C is a central east-to-west connecting corridor system, including a straight staircase connecting

all the floors of working space and a series of vertical light shafts. Sufficient daylight creates a pleasant communication place for all the professors and students. Research workshops, which form the main body of the building, cover all the upper floors to the south of the corridor. Supervisors' studios/flexible workshops and vertical circulation/service units are arranged as two volumes plugged in at different heights to the north of the corridor, with three overlapping voids in between (two indoor planted atriums in the basement and on the second floor, and a roof garden on the sixth floor). They share a common transparent glass envelope on the north façade. A waterfall and stepped planting incorporated into the sunken garden to the south provide a vivid recreational space adjacent to the underground gallery. The overlapping of large-scale public space from north to south produces intense variation in the spatial dimensions and orientation, and intertwines inside with outside. The building becomes the "filter" of the whole environment. In order to interact

2. View from southwest

3. Site map

4. View from southeast

with the environment and demonstrate its interior mechanism, the architects sought to express the visibility of the interior space and the specific surface materials instead of concentrating on the unity of the exterior façade. Different types of spaces have been distinguished in the forms and materials of the façade, making each surface of the building respond to a different context of the site.

(All pictures supplied by project architects. Photographer: Zhang Siye, except Fig 7 by Zhang Min, Fig 17 by Zhou Wei, and Fig 19 by Zhang Bin.)

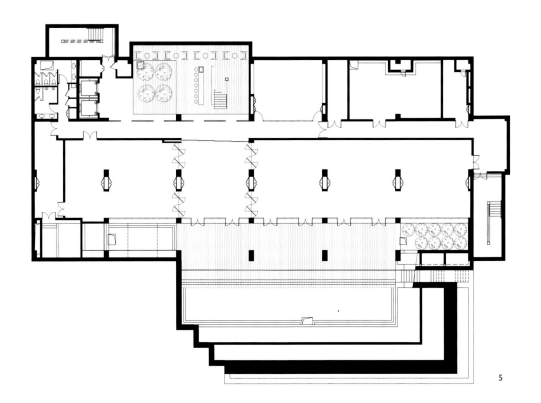

5

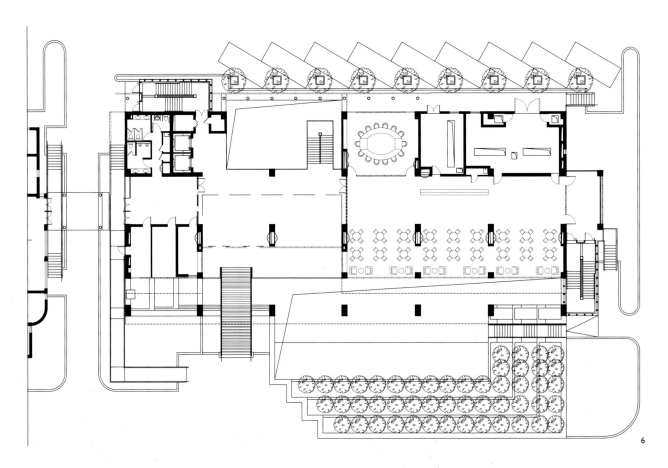

6

5. Basement

6. Ground floor

7. Entrance and sunken garden

8. 6th floor

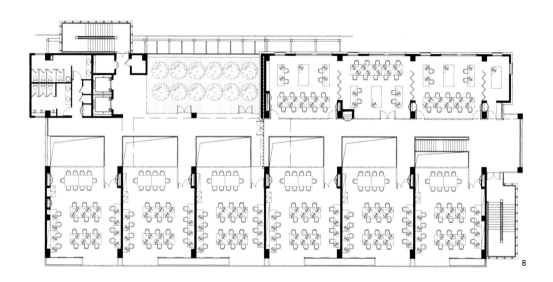

9

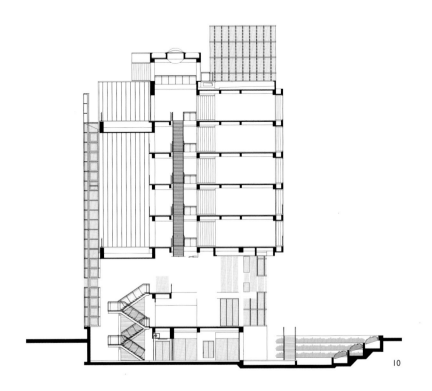

10

9. South elevation

10. Section

11. Entrance hall

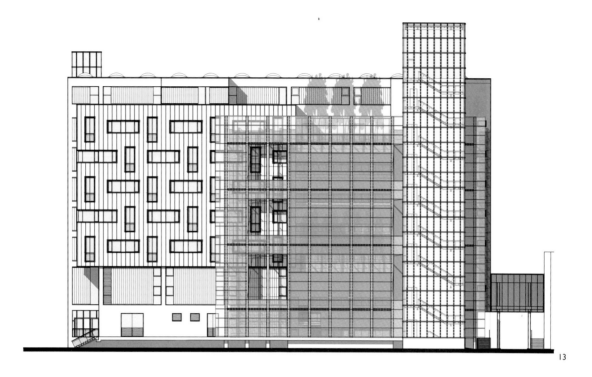

13

12. Staircase

13. North elevation

14. Longitudinal section

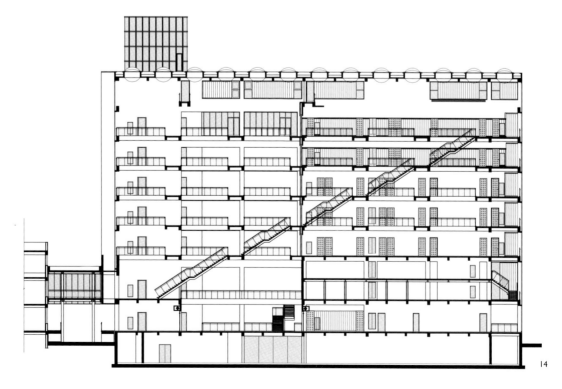

14

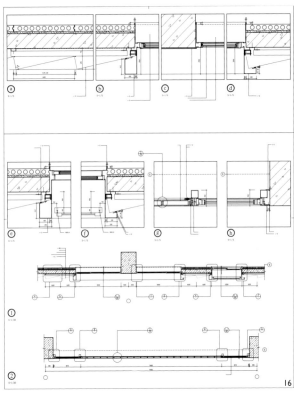

16

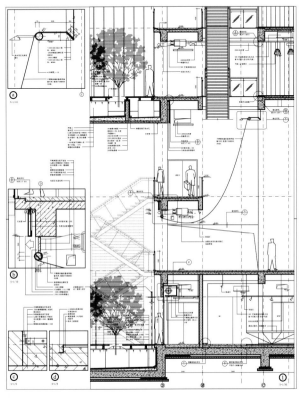

15. Interior courtyard

16. Detail of glass profile unit and stainless steel cladding

17. Corridor on 6th floor

18. Detail section of entrance hall and atrium

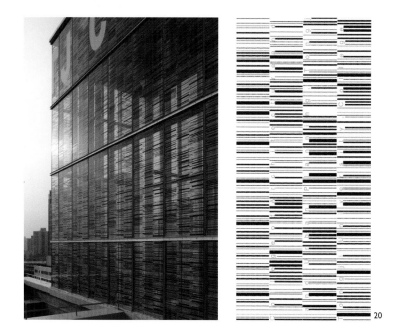

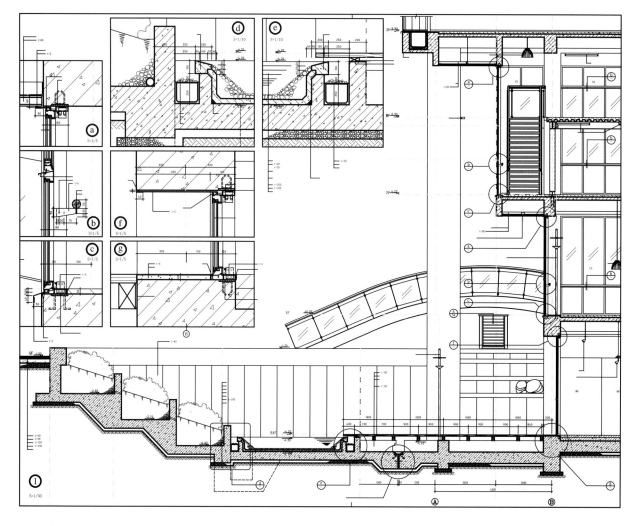

Wuyi Elementary School Auditorium, Beijing

Architect: Standard Architecture

Location: Tongzhou, Beijing
Design / Completion: 2002 / 2004
Area: 2,000 sqm
Architects: Zhang Ke, Zhang Hong, Bu Xiaojun, Li Changle
Client: Wuyi Elementary School, Beijing

The new auditorium has a seating capacity of 520 and is for the use of both the school and the residents of the adjacent neighbourhood. The hall is used for stage performances, films and school events. The auditorium is separated from the main school building by a rectangular courtyard. The school is an unobtrusive four-storey block, against which the expressive form of the auditorium forms a strong contrast. Its characteristic folded red roof makes it a striking feature of the neighbourhood.

The rear wall and the façade form part of the roof, which is supported on both sides by a row of columns. The resulting galleries have walls of red brick into which the wheelchair ramps and the stairs have been integrated. The ground floor on the west side of the building is recessed. The foyer beneath the overhanging roof receives daylight from both sides through its glass wall.

The entrance pierces the vertical wall which rises from the ground as a continuation of the folded roof profile and marks the entrance like a massive sign; the roof is an ironic allusion to the debate that has been going on for decades about the integration of tradition in modern Chinese architecture.

(All pictures supplied by project architects.)

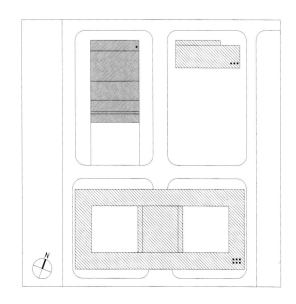

1. Northwest view

2. Site plan

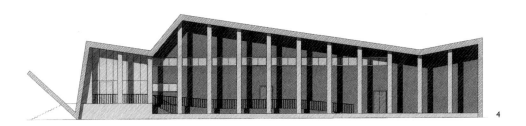

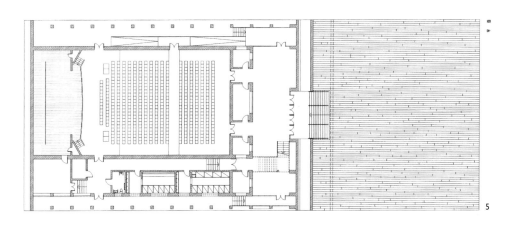

3. Southwest view

4. East elevation

5. Plan

6. Colonnades

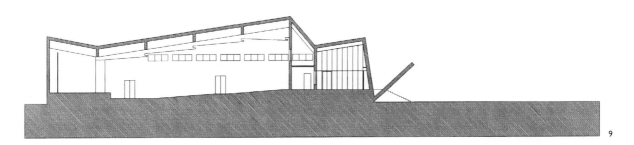

Mandarin Palace, Shanghai

Architect: Rocco Yim

Location: Pudong, Shanghai
Design / Completion: 2003 / 2004
Area: 28,722 sqm
Architect: Rocco Yim
Client: Zendai Group

1. View from Zhang Jia Bang River

Chinese culture is always closely linked with the concept of family in the minds of Chinese people, who treasure unity and harmony. In a family, there are differences between old and young; male and female. The typical forms of residential architecture include the four-sided courtyard in Northern China, private gardens in the area south of the Yangtze River, or walled villages in southern China. Though adjusted to local climate and custom, these building types basically share the same concepts, relating to the idea of family.

While the customers of Shanghai Mandarin Palace are magnates and middle-class families in the 21st century, the traditional concept "respect for the old, love for the young" is deeply rooted. Therefore, the project is seemingly an experiment in Chinese contemporary art, but is, in fact, an interpretation of traditional family concepts. Especially as viewed in terms of space arrangements, the project provides a modern response to traditional family relations.

The Mandarin Palace is located in the Pudong area of Shanghai, close to Century Park. Bounded on two sides by roads and on one side by a river, the site is flat land, where natural landscape is limited. The general layout embodies the typical relationship between buildings and water bodies in villages and towns in the southern Yangtze River area. Drawing water from the southern river onto the site, a meandering water channel divides the site into several peninsulas. Water channels, driveways and alleyways criss-cross the site, connecting houses, streets and the river.

With respect to the design of individual buildings, the Mandarin Palace inherits the traditional concept and craftsmanship of civilian houses in the southern Yangtze River area, with reference to the feeling and atmosphere highlighted by the spatial sequence, brightness contrast and the usage of materials. Regarding the design, the architects discarded traditional symbols and forms, and instead selected modern materials and construction methods, indicative of the times we live in.

From long ago, in the layout of Chinese architecture, whether a palace or a civilian house, interior and exterior spaces are always arranged around courtyards, which creates a comfortable living environment. This concept embodies some old/new principles in various ways, such as privacy protection, clear function division, microclimate condition adjustment, appropriate lighting and ventilation, and warmth in winter and coolness in summer. Above all, the occupants are connected harmoniously with nature, and the courtyards and the houses complement each other, providing people with a well balanced living environment.

Based on the above concept – zoning the plan using walls – the Mandarin Palace places the main courtyards along the central axis, with other courtyards alongside. Buildings with different functions such as the main hall, master bedroom, living room, and other bedrooms are set up around these courtyards, to give each courtyard a specific function.

Another feature of traditional civilian houses is the natural lighting in the interior spaces. In the southern Yangtze River area, thanks to the comfortable climate, it is more appropriate to enhance the transparency of the building. Natural light, introduced from the courtyard, filters into the hall through the tubular eaves, making the light soft and even. The light filters down from above into the small patio beside the reading room or bedroom, which is learned from the customary technique of building domestic houses. The building structure is made of different natural materials displaying different textures, which make interesting light and shadow effects in the spaces.

The design of the façade and the spaces within the Mandarin Palace adopt these elements: skylights, patios, courtyards, stone walls and sun-shading facilities, which reflect the simplicity, elegance, serenity and harmony of traditional houses.

(All pictures supplied by project architects.)

2. House, bamboo and water

3. Exterior facade

4. Outer courtyard

5. Masterplan

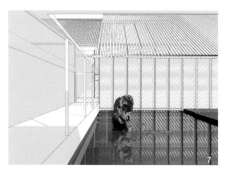

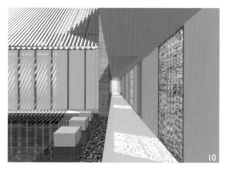

6. Inner courtyard

7. 8. 9. 10. Spatial concept

11. Ground floor plan of Unit A1

12.13. Sections of Unit A1

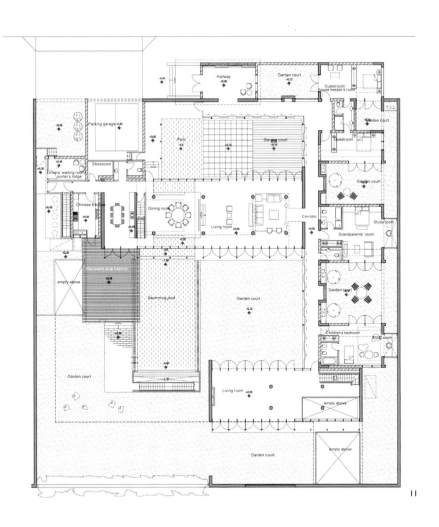

Hallway +0.00
Garden court -0.15
Guestroom/ house keeper's room
Garden court
Parking garage -0.45
Pool -0.5
Garden court -0.15
Guestroom
Storeroom
Drivers' waiting room porter's lodge
Chinese Kitchen
Dining room
Garden court
Living room +0.00
Corridor
Study room
Grandparents' room
empty above
Swimming pool
Garden court -0.15
Garden court
Children's bedroom
Study room
Garden court
Living room +0.00
empty above
Garden court
empty above

11

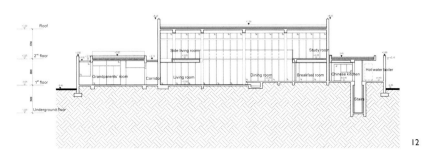

Roof
2nd floor
1st floor
Underground floor
Grandparents' room
Corridor
Side living room
Living room
Dining room
Breakfast room
Chinese kitchen
Study room
Hot water boiler
Stairs

12

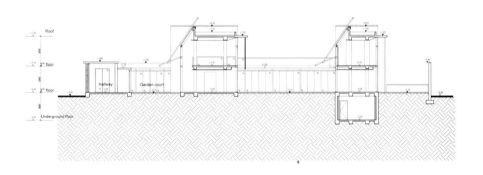

Roof
2nd floor
2nd floor
Underground floor
Hallway
Garden court

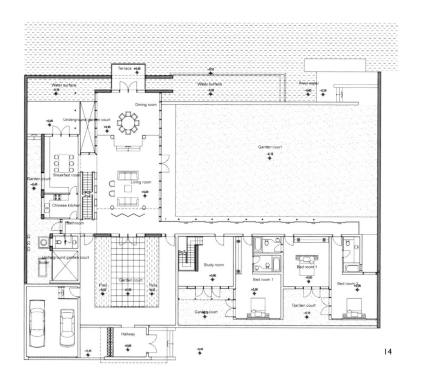

14

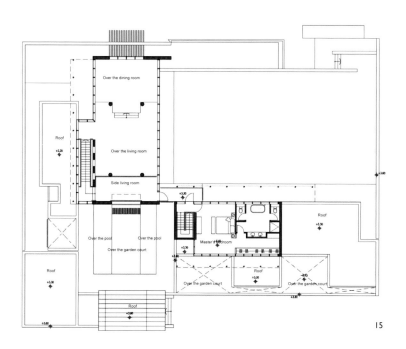

15

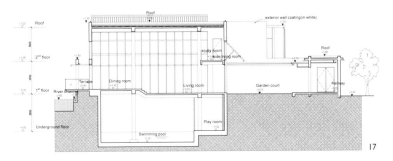

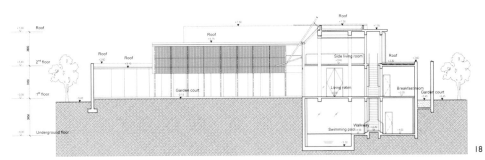

14. Ground floor plan of Unit A4
15. 1st floor plan of Unit A4
16. Night view of outer courtyard
17.18. Sections of Unit A4

Shi Zi Lin Private Club, Beijing

Architect: Zhang Yonghe

Location: Changpin District, Beijing

Design / Completion: 2001.06 / 2003.06

Area: 4,800 sqm

Architect: Zhang Yonghe

The Shi Zi Lin Private Club is located in an orchard in the Wanniangfen Village, Shisanling Town, Changping District, Beijing. In the orchard, many flourishing persimmon trees are planted in orderly rows. Surrounded by hills to the west and the south, the orchard adjoins the village to the north, and faces open spacious woods to the east. Water forms a pond, and the orchard enjoys a natural appearance. The club is built as private villa in which members can entertain relatives and friends.

It is said that the persimmon trees on the site are almost 100 years old, and the owner does not allow any removal of the trees. Therefore, the design of the building must take account of the trees. The inner courtyards surrounding the persimmon trees are dispersed throughout the building, which breaks up the integrity and the logic of the architectural syntax, and forces it to become more open to the environment. The nine "view-finder" rooms that are composed of diagonal walls and sloping roofs are inserted on purpose in the

original rectangular co-ordinate system of the architecture. The rooms not only make openings in the elaborately structured interior spaces, but also interrupt the consistency and continuity of the architectural syntax, which provides views with spatial experiences. All these spatial experiences with their various natures are pieced together, heightening the complexity and the inconsistency of the architecture. The roofing system is mainly designed in a continuously topological configuration that is similar to the roofing structure of traditional Chinese architecture, which is not related to the functions of the building, or the syntactic logic of the covered space. The design of the roofing system is deliberately inconsistent with the whole architectural syntax, which creates many "spectacles" in the interior spaces. For example, the ceiling of the corridor in front of the master bedroom is abruptly interposed by the V-shaped roof, which is unexpected and exciting for the occupants.

Comparing the spatial characteristics between Chinese

1. Site plan
2. Northwest view

architecture and western architecture, Zhang Yonghe has his own opinion. He considers Western architecture to be material, with spaces extended outwards, according to the rules of perspective; while Chinese architecture is non-material, with spaces surrounded, and more often breaking the rules of perspective. The Shi Zi Lin Private Club can hardly be regarded as a material body. Leaving aside that the view of the architecture is blocked by the flourishing persimmon trees, viewers would not be provided with a complete picture of the building's exterior image even if the views were not hindered. The four façades are not consistent with each other and, even individually, none of them is integrated and continuous. Resembling a group, yet not a group, and seeming to be as a whole, yet not a whole, the building does not comply with the usual exterior forms.

It is the interior spaces of the club that really attract the viewers. Specifically, they are attracted by the "circle-in-circle spaces", as well as the spatial experiences of walking among these spaces. "Surrounding" and "circling" are key concepts. In the public spaces of the building, a path made up of small circles loops around the bamboos; in the area of the master bedroom, sitting room and reading room, a route of vertical circles is built to connect the ground floor with the first floor; while in the area of the guestrooms in the north, two connected circles are set up in the upper and lower levels respectively; in the big circle, small courtyards with persimmon trees are inserted, which generates many smaller circles. These nested circles provide viewers with unlimited circulation possibilities, which leads to as many illusions as possible about combinations. In these spaces, both the floor plan and the rule of perspective are rendered invalid.

(All pictures supplied by project architects. Fig 2, 3-5, 6, 7, 10-12, and 14 photographed by Zhi Wenjun; Fig 20, 21 by Shiyi; and Fig 15-19 by Fuxing.)

3.4. South view

5. Axonometric drawing of topological roof

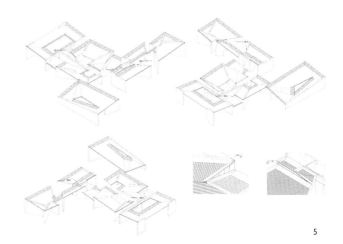

6

7

6. 8. Interior space and courtyard

7. 1st floor plan

9. Ground floor plan

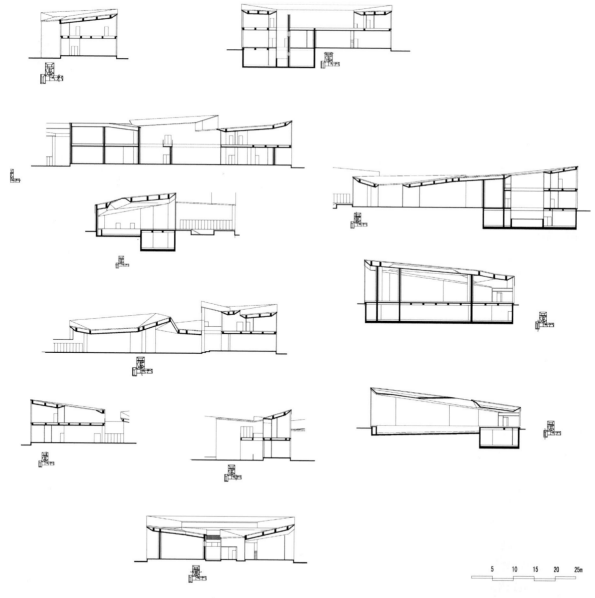

5   10   15   20   25m

Postscript and Acknowledgements

It is quite an arduous task to pick the most influential and significant projects from the immense amount of contemporary Chinese architecture. We hold firmly to the academic spirit of "modernity, foresight, critical thinking" of Times Architecture. We have tried our best to select projects that reveal the architects' basic understanding of local history and culture from different points of view and which at the same time positively reflect the rapid development of contemporary Chinese architecture. We insisted on the principles of personal experience and actual evaluation before publishing to ensure the quality of each project.

The editors who participated in this book are mainly from Times Architecture. They are Dai Chun (Assistant Editor), Zhang Xiaochun (Editor), Ling Lin (Editor), Yao Yanbin (Part-time Editor), Guo Hongxia (Part-time Editor), Xu Diyan (English Editor) and Gu Jinhua (Graphic Executor). They really deserve honour for their precise and painstaking working attitude.

We must specially thank the clients and the architectural teams or architects who designed the buildings and all the staff who have contributed their energy to this book. Their supply of the basic information guarantees the success of this book.

Finally we will say a big thank you to Mr Chen Ciliang and the other editors in Liaoning Science & Technology Publishing House who have contributed a lot to this book.